KU-408-083

Kate Reid

LUNE

Croissants All Day, All Night

PHOTOGRAPHY BY PETE DILLON

Hardie Grant

BOOKS

Introduction 7

RECIPES

I didn't start out my professional life as a pastry chef, and certainly not as a writer, so having this opportunity to reminisce over the many wonderful pastries that have graced the menu since Lune's founding in 2012 has allowed me a deliciously indulgent trip down memory lane, reliving not only some of my favourite pastries, but also special moments attached to their particular era in Lune's brief but wonderful history.

A framed certificate hanging on my wall at home reminds me that I am a qualified Aerospace Engineer, a degree that once meant something very important and specific to me. For the longest time I dreamt of working in Formula One. I was 13 years old when my dad first took me to the Australian Grand Prix. The memories that linger most vividly from that day are the speed and the sound of the cars, that distinctive scream of the V10 engines tearing through the air. I'd never experienced anything like it. I wanted to be on the inside of this world of ground-breaking technical innovation; high risk, but with it, high reward. Not just inside it, I wanted to be a part of it, in fact, *instrumental* to it. The bar was set exceedingly high. But I love a good challenge.

And rise to that challenge I did. I spent five years with my head down, studying for an Aerospace Engineering degree at RMIT University, discovering a fascination and proclivity for aerodynamics, which led me to the hallowed Williams F1 Team. At the tender age of 23 years old, I packed up my life and launched my career as an engineer in the rare air of Formula One.

At the time I didn't know that this was a huge, yet necessary detour. My analytical, process driven, problem-solving mind was meant for a different kind of application. But, had I not possessed a passion for Formula One, I guarantee you, Lune would not be Lune. Precision and innovation run in the veins of the business. At its heart is the relentless pursuit of excellence. Every day we are driven by increasing our knowledge through continuous education and experimentation. We are a croissant Formula One team.

KATE REID

THIS BOOK IS DEDICATED TO LILY

INTRODUCTION

Before staging at Du Pain et des Idèes I had never made croissants before. So my first ever experience with croissants happened to be in one of Paris' most celebrated boulangeries. I returned to Melbourne, inspired by what I had learned at DPDI, and twice attempted croissants at home. Both efforts could only be described as incredibly frustrating, and ultimately, not particularly successful. It seemed that what I had learned in Paris was difficult to translate to the home kitchen.

Soon after these two attempts to produce croissants at home, I made the interesting (some might have argued, questionable) decision to open a bakery that made *only* croissants. I purchased the dough mixer, the laminator, the prover. Bakery established, I clearly remember the day I stood at the bench, the freshly mixed dough in front of me, making the terrifying realisation that I didn't actually know what to do next. During my stage at DPDI I had probably learned only 10–20% of the croissant-making process. There weren't just gaps in my knowledge; there were chasms. But I had signed the lease on the shop, spent my life's savings on the equipment and quit my job, so there was really only one option – fill in the chasms and teach myself. So began a three-month process where I essentially reverse engineered the croissant, eventually landing on a method that was notably different to any other croissant recipe I'd come across. The Lune Croissant was born.

When I signed the contract to write this book, I assumed the recipe for the plain croissant was going to be straightforward. I mean, I'd been making croissants for almost 10 years at Lune, so surely I possessed the knowledge required to write the recipe for the home cook. I started by asking the chefs at Lune to make some extra dough for me, so I could begin testing the laminating process at home, the main difference being with a rolling pin and not a laminator. What ensued was weeks of frustration, endless testing, moments of self-doubt; really questioning whether I actually had the capacity to deliver this recipe. Metaphorically, I felt like I had wound back the clock 10 years, and found myself with all the equipment and ten per cent of the knowledge. Why wasn't it working for me?

But if I could solve this problem once, if I could use my engineering approach and break it down into reading, research, knowledge building, testing and experimentation, maybe I could repeat history. I cast my mind back to those two attempts at making croissants at home, and how difficult it had been. The constant feeling that I wasn't actually sure if I was doing the right thing; the dough felt weird, the pastry was hard to work. The level of detail in the recipes I was following, so lacking that I had no frame of reference as to whether I was on the right track, or I'd veered dangerously off-piste. I remembered that feeling and made a promise that I was going to write a recipe that gave the home cook a fighting chance, a recipe that acknowledged the challenge and frustration, but gently guided the reader through each of the challenging steps.

I finally acknowledged that I couldn't simply take the Lune croissant dough recipe and adapt the laminating process for the home kitchen. I needed to completely change the dough itself.

The method I am about to share with you is not the classic French technique for making croissants. Nor is it how we make croissants at Lune. Let me pre-warn you; this is not for the faint hearted. It requires time, preparation, patience and commitment to following the process. The method I will outline, step by step, is highly unorthodox, but I promise you, it will result in a great end product.

NOTES ON INGREDIENTS

While many different ingredients are used in the recipes that follow, there are a few key components that require a little informative discussion. Not all croissants are created equal, and that starts with your selection of ingredients.

FLOUR

At Lune we make the croissant dough with Laucke Euro, a flour developed specifically for viennoiserie.

The Laucke Euro flour is made up of a unique blend of complimentary wheat varieties, resulting in a set of balanced dough characteristics. For our purposes, the most important properties are the protein content and ash level. Laucke Euro flour has a targeted protein content of 12.3% and ash level of 0.5-0.55%.

The challenge of sourcing the best flour for this croissant dough recipe is that there is no globally agreed upon, standardised set of properties by which flour is defined. Hence if you are planning to embark on my croissant recipe, when sourcing the best flour, try to find a high quality bread, 'high Protein' flour, or more specifically, a 'long ferment/viennoiseries' flour. If the properties of the flour are listed on the packaging, check to make sure the protein content is at least 11.5% and the ash level is in the range 0.48 – 0.58%.

If you are based in Australia, the Laucke Wallaby flour is readily available in supermarkets, and will be a good substitute. For other regions, the following flour mills produce high quality flour and you should be able to speak to them about an appropriate substitute flour:

UK: Shipton Mill (shipton-mill.com)
USA: Central Milling (centralmilling.com)
Germany: Cramer Muehle (cramermuehle.de)
Switzerland: Grueninger Muehlen (grueningermuehlen.ch)
Japan: Masufun Flour Mill (masufun.co.jp)

BUTTER

I could write a whole book on butter (now, there's an idea...). For now, I'll keep it short and relevant.

Buy the very best quality butter you can get your hands on. Full stop.

If nothing else, croissants are truly a reflection of the butter with which they were made. You are going to dedicate at least three days to this pursuit, so honour the process and source great butter.

My croissant recipe incorporates butter in two stages; the croissant dough contains clarified butter, then there is obviously the butter used to laminate into the dough to create the layers in the pastry.

For both of these applications, source organic cultured butter with a minimum fat content of 82%. Cultured butter has a more complex flavour profile than regular butter, it has an acidity that comes from the cultures that are introduced to the cream which is then allowed to ferment. This imparts a nutty quality, and sometimes even natural sweetness. Cultured butter also has a slightly higher melting point than regular butter, which is a property you will be enormously grateful for during the lamination process!

For all other recipes that include butter, regular unsalted butter will be satisfactory.

CLARIFIED BUTTER

Several recipes call for clarified butter, so I thought it pertinent to supply a little introduction to clarified butter and how to make it.

Clarified butter is the pure butterfat, separated from the milk solids and water contained in butter through a process of melting and boiling the butter, such that the water evaporates and the milk solids separate and settle at the bottom of the pan.

To clarify butter, begin by placing the butter in a saucepan and let it melt over a medium heat, then allow it to come to a gentle boil. When a foam begins to form on the surface this indicates that the milk proteins are separating from the butterfat (the foam is made up of milk proteins). Keep boiling the butter gently until the foam dissipates and the bubbles slow down. The slowing down of the bubbles indicates that the water has boiled off. There will be burnt milk solids at the bottom of the pan. Strain the clarified butter, separating the butterfat from the milk solids, by lining a sieve with muslin cloth or a chux (if you're into brewing your own coffee at home, a coffee filter will work too), reserving the pure butterfat liquid and discarding the burnt milk solids.

When clarifying butter, you lose approximately 25% of the original volume, so if a recipe calls for a specific amount of clarified butter, divide the amount of clarified butter by 0.75 to determine the amount of butter you need to start with.

If you're super organised and have clarified butter days before you plan to make croissants, once the strained butterfat cools slightly, but is still in liquid form, weigh the exact amount required for the dough into a heatproof container and allow it to re-solidify, then store in the fridge until you need it.

BROWN BUTTER (BEURRE NOISETTE)

Brown butter is essentially clarified butter, taken further to allow the butterfat to develop a golden-brown hue, imparted by the caramelising milk solids. If a recipe calls for brown butter, follow the above instructions for clarifying butter, but allow it to deepen further in colour before removing from the heat and straining. Brown butter, as per its French name 'beurre noisette', allows the butter to develop a deep toasty, nutty flavour.

EGGS

All recipes that include eggs call for large eggs. One large egg weighs approximately 55g, including the shell. Without the shell, the egg weighs approximately 50g, the yolk component comprising 20g and the white 30g.

Where possible, source organic, free-range eggs.

MILK

Whole milk (full fat) is the only option, for all recipes.

YEAST

The croissant dough recipe includes fresh compressed yeast (otherwise known as fresh yeast or cake yeast). Fresh compressed yeast normally has an advertised shelf-life of 4 weeks from date of production. At Lune we will not use yeast with less than 3 weeks of shelf life remaining. While it is one of the least expensive ingredients used in the production of the croissant dough, variation and unpredictability in the activity level of yeast can have the greatest negative effect on the finished product, which you won't fully discover until you attempt to bake the croissants on the third day.

Source the yeast from a trusted supplier; often specialty ingredients stores will stock yeast. I would recommend asking for the use-by date for the particular batch of yeast you are purchasing, and look for a light beige colour and a dry, crumbly texture.

CHOCOLATE BATONS

If you can get your hands on proper 'bâtons boulanger', they are already shaped with the perfect length and weight for a pain au chocolat. If you can't get chocolate batons, fear not, literally any semi-sweet chocolate can be used. I would recommend a chocolate with a minimum of 44% cacao for that slightly bitter dark chocolate flavour. It pairs beautifully with the buttery pastry.

GELATINE

All recipes that require gelatine are referring to gold-strength gelatine leaves, which need to be soaked in cold water for up to 10 minutes, until soft (known as blooming the gelatine), then the excess water should be gently wrung out of the leaves before adding them to the warmed liquid you wish to set.

VANILLA

The recipes call for vanilla in a few different forms, but you can substitute based on availability of the different types of vanilla.

The seeds of one vanilla pod
=
1 tablespoon vanilla bean paste
=
1 tablespoon vanilla extract

If you are making a recipe where the seeds will be visible in the finished product (for example, vanilla crème pâtissière), I would recommend using the seeds from a vanilla pod or vanilla bean paste. The Salted Chocolate Chip Cookies (page 231) however, do not require the visual of the vanilla bean seeds, only the flavour of vanilla, so extract is sufficient.

Store vanilla pods in a snap-lock bag or airtight container in the fridge. Don't throw out pods that have had the seeds scraped from them – they are still great for adding to a poaching liquid or infusing sugar with vanilla scent and flavour!

NOTES ON EQUIPMENT

If you are a frequent home baker, I would put money on the fact that your kitchen is probably already kitted out with the equipment required to make croissants. Basically, it boils down to a stand mixer, a rolling pin, a ruler and a sharp knife. Got all of that? Then you're good to go! The following list will just make your life a whole lot easier ...

DIGITAL KITCHEN SCALES

At Lune, we meticulously weigh everything to the gram. To some, that may seem overkill, but it is my opinion that if you cut one corner, it's a slippery slope and your tolerance for error will only increase. It is important to remember that baking is as much of a science as it is food preparation, and the ratio of ingredients is a critical factor in the finished product turning out as it was intended.

In baking (and in life) if you're going to do something, the philosophy I live by is to do it to the very best of your ability. If you are serious about home baking, I would highly recommend purchasing a set of digital kitchen scales accurate to the gram (with a 'tare' function). If you are a coffee afficionado, you may also be in possession of a set of espresso scales, typically accurate to 0.1g. These can be particularly useful when it comes to weighing spices, gelatine and other leavening agents such as baking powder or bicarbonate of soda.

STAND MIXER

A stand mixer is a crucial piece of kitchen equipment, required in many of the recipes in this book. You will need a stand mixer that includes the following attachments:

- Flat beater
- Whisk
- Dough hook

In 2009, my parents gave me a KitchenAid stand mixer for my birthday. 13 years later, including 2 solid years of a daily thrashing at Lune, it's still going strong. I could not recommend a KitchenAid more highly.

ROLLING PIN

Upon embarking on writing this book I received some pretty excellent rolling pin advice from my Head Chef, Chloe. Simple is best. For the laminating of the croissant dough, I recommend using a dowel, which is a straight wooden rolling pin with a continuous diameter, as it allows you to apply even and consistent pressure when rolling out the pastry. A French tapered rolling pin would work too. My recipe for making croissant pastry works in small batch sizes, so a smaller rolling pin will give you greater control when working the pastry (and frankly, it's just easier to use!).

If your rolling pin is wooden, simply wipe it clean with a damp cloth, don't submerge it in water. The wood will absorb the water, which can warp the rolling pin.

KNIVES AND OTHER SHARP THINGS

If you are going to attempt making croissants at home, you will require access to several sharp implements:

- Paring knife: critical for marking out the different shapes to be cut from a batch of pastry

- Chef's knife: cutting the different shapes from a batch of pastry requires a large sharp-bladed knife

- Pizza wheel: different shapes of pastry can also be cut using a pizza wheel (as we do at Lune)

- Serrated bread knife: required for twice-baked croissant preparation

RULER

For the laminating of the dough and the final marking and cutting of batches you will require a ruler of at least 40 cm (16 in). It is useful to have access to a tape measure during the laminating process too.

PASTRY BRUSH

Not all pastry brushes are created equal, and most of the proceeding recipes call for qualities in a pastry brush specific to egg washing proven pastries. The ideal pastry brush has a wide, flat head of soft bristles (at Lune we use a brush with a head approximately 4 cm/1½ in wide and bristles 3 cm/1 in long). This ensures good coverage of egg wash with each stroke, the soft bristles minimising damage to the delicate surface of the proven pastry (note that damage is only avoided entirely with a gentle touch!)

Try to source a brush with bristles made from natural fibres (as opposed to plastic or silicone). The natural fibre bristles hold egg wash well, meaning the egg wash won't easily fall out of the bristles and pool around the proven pastry (this tends to result in a 'burnt omelette' around the bottom of the pastry).

Caring for your pastry brush; after use, make sure you rinse the egg out of the brush thoroughly with cold water, before using any detergent or hot water. Rinsing first with hot water will cook the residual egg nestled within the bristles.

OFFSET PALETTE KNIFE ('CRANKED SPATULA')

I would recommend having two different sizes of offset palette knives – a smaller one with a blade of approximately 10 cm (4 in), great for more detailed work, such as spreading custards or fillings on the raw pastry for escargot assembly, and a larger one with a blade of 20 cm (8 in), useful for lifting just-baked pastries or flipping kouign-amann mid-bake.

DRUM SIEVE

Not only required for its obvious function of sifting dry ingredients, passing a slightly grainy or lumpy custard through a drum sieve can rescue the custard. You can also use one for making incredibly light and fluffy mashed potato.

PIPING BAGS

Many of the recipes in this book require piping (pastry) bags, two different types are referenced:

- Large reusable piping bags, fitted with specific nozzles, are great for piping frangipane, which has a fairly firm consistency. Once transferred into the piping bag, it will not run out of the open nozzle.

- Small disposable piping bags, where a nozzle is not required, are best for fillings and garnishes that have a more liquid consistency, and for when you need to keep the tip of the piping bag sealed until it is time to use it. You also have greater control over the exact size of the opening in the tip of the piping bag. They are available in most supermarkets in the cake decorating aisle, or any specialty baking store.

TINS AND OTHER IMPORTANT BITS OF KIT

If you're going to bake anything (from this book or in life in general), you'd be well placed to have one or two wire cooling racks in the cupboard.

All the escargot shaped pastries utilise 11 cm (4½ in) round springform tins. I would strongly suggest sourcing some of these tins, because, trust me, you are going to want to give the escargot recipes a go. Most leading bakeware manufacturers produce a springform tin of this size.

Cruffins are proven and baked in a loose-based dessert pan that has been greased and lined with baking paper, so they don't stick to the sides of the tin and can be easily popped out of the baking pan. You can also use a muffin tin if you don't have a dessert pan, but keep in mind that the tapered edges of the muffin tin will result in a different-looking end product.

It's worthwhile having a set of 6 cm (2½ in) square silicone moulds in your artillery, as all the blind baked danish recipes call for them. Again, they can be sourced relatively easily at specialist bakeware stores, or online.

THE RAW PASTRY

Day 1: AM
Poolish

Day 1: PM
Croissant dough

Day 2: AM
Lamination

Day 3
Baking

Poolish

A poolish is a type of liquid pre-ferment used in making bread and yeasted pastry. At Lune we do not make a poolish, but in this method for the home kitchen it is necessary. Laminating the dough (creating the multiple layers of dough and butter through the process of rolling out and folding the pastry) with a dough sheeter (laminator), works the dough far more gently than hand laminating with a rolling pin. The main purpose of the poolish in this application is to increase the extensibility (or stretchiness) of the dough, essentially making it easier to roll out by hand. It also has the wonderful added benefit of increasing the complexity of flavour of the final product, encouraging more nuttiness and acidity, the likes of which you would find as a lovely subtle 'tang' in good sourdough bread.

Milk	300 g
Water	70 g
Fresh yeast	2 g
Flour	370 g

1   Put the milk and water in a small saucepan, and over a low heat, gently take the chill off the milk. You do not want to heat the milk, you just want to bring it to room temperature. Test the temperature of it with your finger – it should not feel cold or warm, just skin temperature. As soon as it has reached this temperature, take the pan off the heat.

2   Crumble the fresh yeast into the milk and water and whisk such that it is completely dissolved.

3   Pour the milk, water and yeast combination into the bowl of your stand mixer fitted with the dough hook attachment, then add the flour.

4   Mix on low speed for 2 minutes. The batter will look a little like thick, shaggy pancake batter. There should be no lumps of unmixed flour. Cover the bowl with cling film and leave at room temperature (21°C/70°C is perfect) for a minimum of 5 hours.

5   In this time your poolish should dramatically increase in volume, and small bubbles will form on the surface. If you are using a standard (4.8-litre) KitchenAid mixing bowl, it will rise approximately halfway up the bowl.

6   Yes, it is possible overprove your poolish. After it has risen to its maximum capacity (the 'high water mark') it will begin to deflate, the batter left clinging to the sides of the bowl. The poolish is ready to use when it has literally *just started to recede* and is no longer forming a dome shape. If you allow your poolish to deflate too much, you'll have to start again.

7   Remember that if the room you are proving the poolish in is warmer than 21°C (70°C), this process may happen quicker than 5 hours, equally if the room is cooler than 21°C (70°C), it may take longer (my kitchen typically sits at around 18°C and the poolish takes 7–8 hours to reach full maturity). So, my advice is – just before the 5-hour mark – start to keep a really close eye on it.

TIP   The most accurate way to weigh your ingredients is to have a set of digital scales with a 'tare' function (i.e. set the mixing bowl on your scales then "tare" the scales, such that they read zero).

Croissant dough

Once your poolish has reached full maturity, it's time to make your croissant dough.

Fresh yeast	54 g
Water	100 g
Flour	865 g
Caster (superfine) sugar	155 g
Table salt	26 g
Eggs	100 g
Clarified Butter	100 g

TIP Chose a container that is just a little bit bigger than your boule of dough (allowing 2–3 cm/ ¾–1 in) gap between the dough and each side of the container). The dough will then naturally prove into a rectangular shape, which will help you immensely in the next step!

1   To make the croissant dough the clarified butter must be in liquid form and warm. If you have pre-clarified your butter and stored it in the fridge, re-melt it in a saucepan over a gentle heat, but make sure to only heat it through, not bring it to the boil. If you're clarifying the butter just before you begin the dough, it's good practice to have the correct amount of clarified butter strained and weighed in a saucepan to keep it warm, prior to starting to weigh the rest of the ingredients, so make sure you do this step first. (For instructions on how to clarify butter see page 10).

2   In a mixing bowl, crumble the fresh yeast into the water, breaking it down as much as you can with your fingers, then whisk the yeast into the water, until it forms a uniform, muddy coloured liquid.

3   Take the bowl of your stand mixer with the poolish and place it on the scales. Add the water and yeast mixture to your poolish, then 'tare' your scales to zero. Now add your flour, sugar, salt and eggs.

4   Attach the dough hook to your stand mixer and mix on the lowest speed for 2 minutes. The dough will still look lumpy and a little floury at this stage. After this phase of the mixing is complete, give the bowl a good scrape down then turn the mixer back on to the lowest speed. Slowly start to pour the warm clarified butter into the mixture, over a period of 2 minutes. Once all the butter is added, increase the mixer speed to medium and mix for 2 minutes. At this stage you have a choice to finish kneading the dough in the mixer, continuing to mix on medium speed for a further two minutes. I, however, prefer to finish the kneading of the dough by hand, as I find I am more in tune with how the dough feels when it is ready (it's also just really relaxing to knead dough!).

5   If you choose to finish the kneading by hand, tip the dough out of the bowl onto a clean benchtop and knead the dough for a further 4–5 minutes, until it is smooth and homogenous. Now, as best you can, fashion your dough into an oblong 'boule', gently creating tension on the surface of the dough by tucking it in, such that any seams or cracks are only on the bottom of the boule. Put the dough in a rectangular container lined with baking paper, then cover it well with cling film, creating a 'second skin' (try to make it airtight – if it is at all exposed to air those little patches of dough will dry out and become crusty), and put it straight into the fridge. It's going to spend the whole night in here, having a lovely long, slow, cold fermentation – this is the time where the dough really develops its beautiful complexity of flavour.

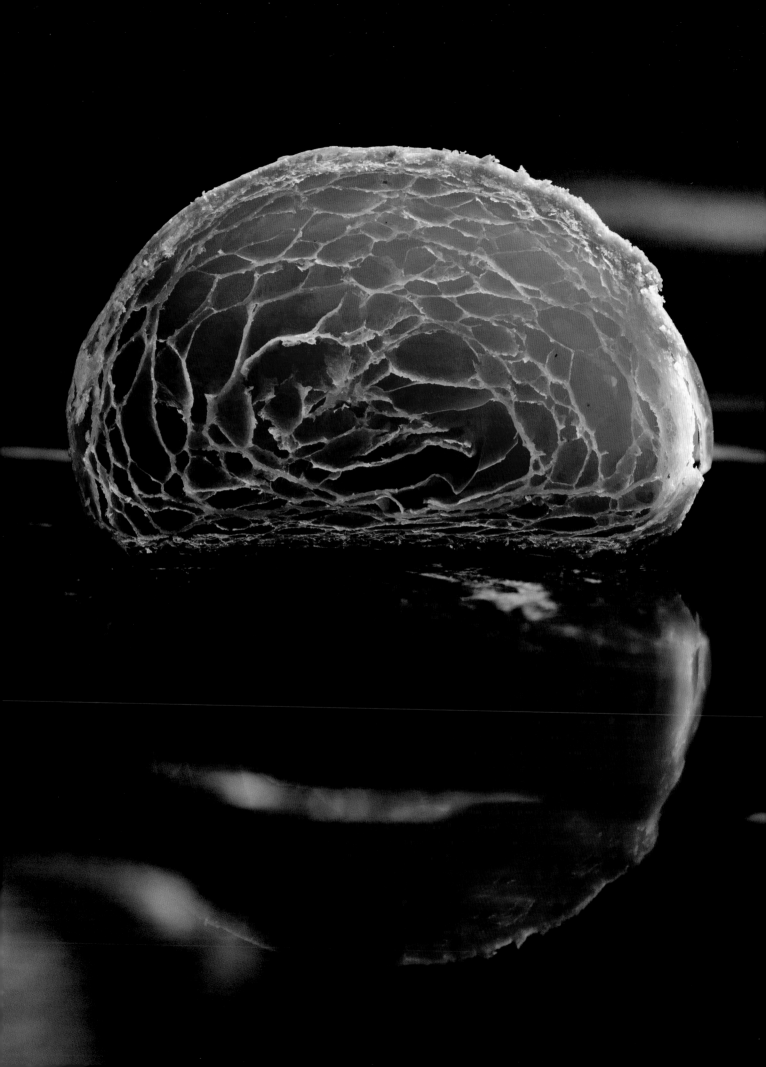

CREATING THE LAYERS

Most recipes don't tell you how hard it is to make croissants at home. At Lune we use a piece of equipment called a laminator (or dough sheeter) to do all the muscle work. The laminator is essentially two large rolling pins, the distance between them controlled mechanically, such that the operator of the laminator can slowly decrease the gap, and gently roll the pastry out progressively thinner and thinner. Don't be fooled; without a laminator this is *really* hard work. When we try to do it by hand with a rolling pin, we impart strength into the dough and develop the gluten. The more we develop the gluten, the more the pastry will want to 'spring back', and it becomes harder and harder to roll out to the dimensions called for in a recipe. It is also really hard to apply even and consistent pressure when using a rolling pin, which is critical when making croissant pastry!

The process of creating the multiple layers of dough and butter in the pastry ('lamination') also requires that the pastry is rested in the fridge between each stage, to relax the gluten and also prevent the butter from melting. Logic also tells us though, that resting the dough in the fridge will firm it up, which again increases the difficulty of rolling it out by hand with a rolling pin.

Finally, pastry that has rested in the fridge will have solid butter layers. We have to be careful that the butter doesn't become *too* solid, such that it cracks and breaks when we are rolling it out – this will result in a break in the layer of butter, and hence inconsistent lamination. So, the suggested timings in the following method should be closely adhered to.

We haven't even touched on the fact that you probably don't have a climate-controlled room in your house, where the temperature and humidity is kept constant, or a chilled benchtop, or proving cabinets.

Are you getting an idea of how challenging this is?

There are some things we do at Lune that are non-negotiable when making croissants. While the technique I outline in this book is far removed from the technique we use at Lune, some of the core principles carry over.

From here on in, do not expect a traditional croissant recipe.

Classically, when making croissant pastry, all of the butter is added at the beginning of the lamination process. The technique I have developed here is different in that it adds the butter in two stages. I have also slightly reduced the quantity of butter laminated into the dough, to make working with the pastry a little easier. Fear not, I haven't actually cut down on total amount of butter in the finished croissants. You will remember that the dough recipe includes clarified butter, which adds complexity to the flavour of the dough and ensures holy levels of butteriness. It's a little trick that will make the process slightly easier at home, without compromising on the final butter flavour of your croissants. You're welcome.

Rest the pastry.

Nothing great comes easy or fast. This is true for pastry too. It is absolutely essential to rest and chill the dough after each stage of the process – each time I recommend you rest your pastry, follow this instruction religiously. I promise I'm not just being a pastry tyrant, I have your ultimate success in mind, and am suggesting this for your own good! Not only will this result in a better end product, it will also minimise the extreme level of frustration you will otherwise feel during the process!

Never sprinkle flour on the benchtop.

This is a technique commonly used to deal with butter that may break through the layers of your pastry and end up on your benchtop, making your pastry greasy, sticky and ultimately incredibly difficult to work with. It is a lazy technique, a bit of a hack. Sprinkling flour on your work surface adds an unknown quantity of flour to your pastry that you have so meticulously weighed out all the ingredients for at the start of the process; indeed, an incredibly inexact and detrimental addition, with undesirable results.

Roll confidently but carefully.

The only way to avoid breaking the outer layer of your pastry (and hence, eliminating the need to sprinkle flour on your work surface) is to treat that outer layer of dough as if it were your first-born child. You are going to do everything in your power to maintain its integrity, because it's the only thing standing between your first layer of sticky, greasy, level-of-difficulty-increasing butter and your benchtop.

Lamination

1 x dough (prepared the day before)	
butter at room temperature	600 g

One of the toughest things about making croissants at home is the laminating process. Yes, we've all used a rolling pin to make shortcrust pastry for a tart. But don't underestimate the challenge of rolling out yeasted dough with well-developed gluten. In order to make the process more achievable, in the following method I propose dividing the dough into four smaller portions and preparing mini batches.

Before removing your dough from the fridge, ensure that your benchtop is cool. If your benchtop is warm, Day 2 is going to be near impossible, and simply result in an incredibly frustrating and unsuccessful day of attempting to make croissants. If you live in a warm climate and your benchtop has a high thermal mass – i.e. concrete, marble, granite – it will probably be quite warm, as these materials absorb and store heat. If it doesn't feel cool to the touch, you will need to cool it down before beginning the next part of the process, and keep it cool while you are working with the raw pastry. This can simply be done by periodically resting bags of frozen peas (or similar) on the section of the benchtop you're using.

The ideal room temperature to work with raw, yeasted pastry is 18°C (65.4°F). Again, if you live in a warm climate, I would recommend cranking the air conditioner (for your pastry, as well as your sanity).

1   Once your benchtop is cool, take your dough out of the fridge. It should have proven such that it is filling the container and has taken on a rectangular shape.

2   Turn your dough out onto the benchtop with the original underside facing up.

3   Using the heels of your hands, gently knock the air out of the dough and fashion it into a rectangle.

40 CM (16 IN)

30 CM (12 IN)

4   You are now going to use your rolling pin to roll out your dough to a rectangle approximately 40 cm (16 in) wide by 30 cm (12 in) deep. I say approximate and I mean it. Don't kill yourself trying to get those exact dimensions. The bigger your rectangle, the easier the rest of the process is going to be, so just use this as a guide.

Working from the middle of the dough outwards, apply even pressure with your rolling pin and gently and progressively increase the size of your dough rectangle. This part of the process cannot be hurried, or sped up with force. It is critical to keep your pressure gentle and even.

5   Once your dough rectangle is approximately 40 × 30 cm (16 × 12 in), carefully transfer your dough to a large baking sheet lined with baking paper, cover well with cling film, and refrigerate for a minimum of 1 hour.

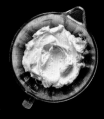

6   Meanwhile, put your room-temperature butter into the bowl of your stand mixer, and with the flat beater attachment, mix the butter on a low-medium speed – be careful not to cream or aerate the butter, you are simply softening it.

10 CM (4 IN)

1 After at least 1 hour's rest in the fridge, take your dough rectangle out. Remove the cling film and transfer the dough to your benchtop. Use a ruler at least 40 cm (16 in) long to mark intervals at 10 cm (4 in), 20 cm (8 in) and 30 cm (12 in) along the top edge of your dough.

2 Repeat the marks at 10cm (4 in) intervals along the bottom edge.

3 Align your ruler with each of the corresponding points (i.e. the 10 cm/4 in mark on the top edge with the 10 cm/4 in mark on the bottom edge).

4 Using a chef's knife cut your dough into four equal strips. These four strips of dough are going to become the four smaller individual batches.

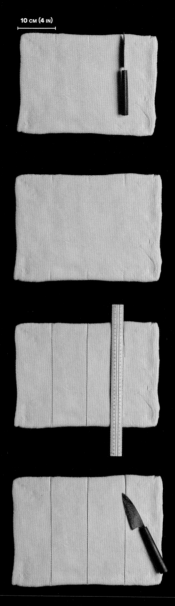

5 Take the first strip of dough and lay it with the long edge running parallel to the edge of your benchtop.

6 Transfer the remaining three strips back to the lined baking sheet, cover with cling film and return to the fridge.

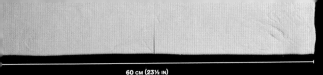

7 Using consistent, even pressure, roll the dough out to a length of 60 cm (23½ in). Score an indent with your knife at the 30 cm (12 in) mark (the midpoint).

60 CM (23½ IN)

8 Place your mixing bowl of softened butter on your digital scales and 'tare' them to zero. Using an offset spatula, take small amounts of butter out of the bowl and dollop it evenly along the right hand half of the dough, until you have a total of 100 g (3½ oz) of butter on the pastry (i.e. the scales are reading -100 g/3½ oz).

9 Using the offset spatula, spread the butter as evenly as you can over half of the dough, leaving a very small border around the edges (2–3 mm maximum).

10 Carefully lift the unbuttered half of the dough over and enclose the buttered half, gently sealing the edges.

11 Wrap this dough/butter preparation in baking paper, then either wrap in clingfilm or transfer t

nd place it with the long edge parallel to the edge
 the benchtop.

   With gentle, even pressure, working from the
iddle of the pastry out, roll the pastry out to a
ngth of 50 cm (19½ in). You may have to flip the
stry over a couple of times in the early part of
is process, such that the bottom side doesn't
come stuck to the benchtop, which will result in
tending the top side of the pastry more than the
derside, and uneven distribution of the butter.
u can also gently feather the pastry off the
nchtop as you are rolling, again to stop it from
cking to the benchtop.

   Once you have rolled your pastry out to
ength of 50 cm (19½ in), use your knife
ore an indent at the 20 cm (8 in) and
 cm (17½ in) marks.

   With your bowl of softened butter on the
ales, take small amounts of butter with your offset
atula, distributing them inside these two marks.

   Once you have 50 g (1¾ oz) of butter on
 pastry, spread the butter out as evenly as
u can, again leaving a small margin at the
ges of the pastry.

   Carefully peeling the right-hand end of the
stry off the benchtop, fold it over such that it
vers one quarter of the buttered area.

   Now repeat this process with the left-hand
d, such that the butter is totally enclosed.
ntly create a join between the two ends of
stry, where they have met in the middle.

   Now pick up the left-hand end and fold it
er to meet the right-hand end, completing the
ok fold'.

Wrap the batch of pastry in baking paper

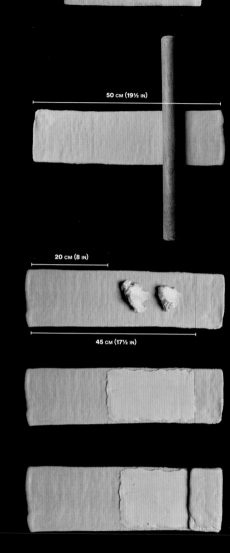

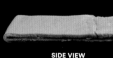

SIDE VIEW

Step 4

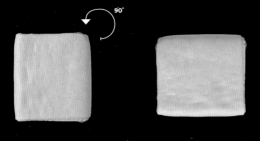

90°

1   Take the first batch of pastry out of the fridge and align the 'spine' of the batch parallel to the edge of the benchtop. By orientating the pastry in this way, you have achieved the required 90 degree rotation.

42 CM (16½ IN)

14 CM (5½ IN)

28 CM (11 IN)

2   You are now going to roll out the pastry to three times the width of the batch. Typically, if you have followed all the steps above closely, the batch of pastry will be approximately 14 cm (5½ in) wide, so you need to roll out the pastry to a length of 42 cm (16½ in). Again, if necessary, flip the pastry a couple of times to avoid it sticking to the benchtop, so you get an even roll out of the top and bottom layers of dough.

3   Take your ruler and, measuring from the left-hand end, score a gentle indent with your knife two thirds along the length of the pastry (28 cm/11 in if the full length of the pastry is measuring as above).

4   Carefully lifting the left-hand end, fold it to the mark you have just made.

5   Now lift the right-hand end and fold it over the top (like how you would fold a business letter).

SIDE VIEW

6   Wrap the batch of pastry in baking paper and transfer back into the Ziplock freezer bag. Rest Batch 1 in the freezer for 30 minutes (set a timer so you don't forget it's in there!)

7   Remove Batch 1 from the freezer after 30 minutes and transfer to the fridge.

CHEF NOTE   For the second 'turn' the batch of pastry is rotated 90 degrees on the benchtop from the orientation it finished the first 'turn' in (this is where the term 'turn' comes from!). When you roll out the pastry for this step, you're developing the gluten strands in a direction perpendicular to the first turn. This is important for extensibility (stretchiness) of the pastry. For this recipe the second turn features a 'letter fold'.

While Batch 1 is resting in the freezer, complete the second turn for the other three batches, repeating steps 1 to 6.

All of the turns have now been completed and the pastry is ready for its final roll out and shaping. At this stage I would highly recommend resting the pastry in the fridge for several hours before attempting the final roll out. This will allow the gluten to relax and make the pastry *much* easier to roll out. Trust me, you're going to be grateful you waited!

You now also need to decide how many of the batches you plan to shape into pastries to bake the following day. Each batch will yield between five and eight pastries of different varieties. If you only want to bake, for example, five traditional croissants, you can keep the remaining three batches in the freezer, for use at a later date. When you are ready to use one of these batches, transfer it from the freezer to the fridge and leave for a minimum of 12 hours (overnight is ideal) to thaw out before completing final roll out and shaping.

THE DIFFERENT SHAPES

So, the good news is, if you've worked your way through the chapter on Raw Pastry, four perfect little batches of laminated pastry are wrapped and resting in your fridge – you've done the hardest work! Now you get to have fun and create some deliciously different Lune pastries.

Each 'mini batch' will yield five to eight pastries, varying depending on the style of pastry you want to make. The following chapter details how to roll out, mark and cut the pastry for each of the different shapes. The recipes in the chapters that follow will reference the information provided in this chapter, so expect these pages to be dog-eared and butter finger-printed.

Please also note that cutting a batch of pastry to achieve any of the following shapes will generate some pastry trim. Have a sealable container handy to reserve the trim and store in the fridge, as it can be used for other recipes in the book.

Croissant

CUTTING

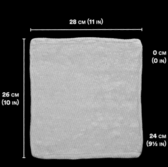
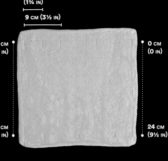
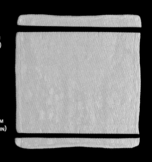

28 cm (11 in)

26 cm (10 in)

4.5 cm (1¾ in)

9 cm (3½ in)

0 cm (0 in)

24 cm (9½ in)

0 cm (0 in)

24 cm (9½ in)

1 Position the batch on the benchtop, such that the 'open ends' of the letter are facing towards you and away from you.

2 Using a rolling pin, roll the pastry out first away from you and toward you until it is at least 26 cm (10 in) deep. Then, working side to side, roll your pastry out, to a width of at least 28 cm (11 in).

3 Position your ruler vertically along the left hand edge of the pastry, marking the 0 cm (0 in) and 24 cm (9½ in) points. Repeat this on the right hand edge of the pastry. Gently score a line across the top of the pastry at the 0 cm (0 in) mark, then make small indents at 0 cm (0 in), 4.5 cm (1¾ in) essentially the midpoint of the first croissant.

4 Line up your ruler with the two 0 cm (0 in) marks at the top of the pastry, then using a sharp knife, cut the top edge of the batch off. Reserve.

Now line up your ruler with the two 24 cm (9½ in) marks at the bottom of the pastry. Using a sharp knife trim off the bottom edge. Reserve.

SHAPING

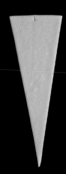

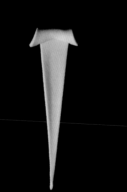

40 cm (16 in)

1 Using a paring knife, make a small nick in the centre of the base of the triangle (approximately 1 cm/ ¾ in).

2 Gently holding the wide base of the triangle in your left hand, confidently, but smoothly, stretch the dough by running your right thumb down the length of the triangle, aiming for a final length of around 40 cm (16 in).

3 Holding either side of the little nick in the base, gently pull the pastry to create a gap where the cut is. By doing this you are essentially making the base of the triangle wider.

4 Working from the wide base of the triangle, roll up the dough towards you with a little tension to ensure that it is tightly rolled.

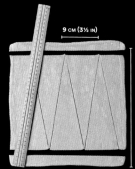

9 cm (3½ in)

24 cm (9½ in)

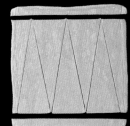

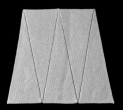

5 As per the image above, mark and cut five triangles, each with a base of 9 cm (3½ in) and a height of 24 cm (9½ in). If you can, allow a little margin from the very edges of the batch.

6 The strips of pastry from the top and bottom of the batch can be reserved to make a cruffin. Store these pieces in the fridge in an airtight container until ready to use.

7 Using the width of your ruler, cut additional strips of pastry that could be used to make a cruffin.

The little left over offcuts should also be reserved as they can be used to make the topping for the Fish Pie recipe!

You should now have five unrolled triangles measuring 9 cm (3 ½ in) at the base, with a height of 24 cm (9½ in), ready to shape!

5 You should be able to achieve three full rolls, and the final point of the triangle should end up on the underside of the shaped croissant.

Press gently to seal the point, so that it does not pop up and unravel during the proving and baking process.

CHEF'S NOTE As the layers of dough and butter are now so thin, the warmth in your hands will melt the butter if you do not perform this series of steps quickly.

Arrange croissants on a baking tray lined with baking paper, with ample distance between each croissant.

At this point the croissants can be reserved in the fridge until it is time to prove them. Carefully cover the tray with cling film to avoid a dry skin forming.

Pain au Chocolat

YIELDS 6, PLUS ONE CRUFFIN

CUTTING

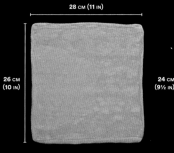
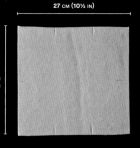
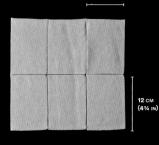

28 CM (11 IN) · 26 CM (10 IN) · 27 CM (10½ IN) · 24 CM (9½ IN) · 9 CM (3½ IN) · 12 CM (4¾ IN)

1 Position the batch on the benchtop, such that the 'open ends' of the letter are facing towards you and away from you.

2 Roll out the pastry exactly as per the 'Croissant Shape' (to at least 26 cm/ 10¼ in deep and 28 cm/ 11 in wide).

3 Using a ruler and a paring knife, mark out a rectangle measuring 27 cm (10½ in) wide and 24 cm (9½ in) deep, allowing for adequate trim on all sides. Cut out the rectangle, reserving all trim for cruffins.

4 As per the image above, mark and cut six rectangles, each with a base of 9 cm (3½ in) and a height of 12 cm (4¾ in).

SHAPING

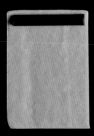

1 Place one chocolate baton along the top (short) edge of each rectangle of pastry. Position the second chocolate baton nearby.

2 Using the tips of your fingers, gently feather the top edge of the pastry off the benchtop, using your thumbs to hold the chocolate baton in place. Fold the top edge of the pastry over, such that the first chocolate baton is now partially rolled up.

3 Place the second chocolate baton on top of the just-folded piece of pastry and, using the palm of your hand, roll the pastry up in one motion, applying no tension, towards yourself.

4 Aim for the join to finish underneath the rolled pastry. Gently press down on the rolled pastry – this will encourage the join, securing the shape, which will prevent the pain au chocolat from unravelling during proving and baking.

Place the six pain au chocolat on a baking tray lined with baking paper, well-spaced to allow for proving and baking. At this point the pains au chocolat can be reserved in the fridge until it is time to prove them. Carefully cover the tray with cling film to avoid a dry skin forming

UTTING

24 CM (9½ IN)

35 CM (13¾ IN)

22 CM (8½ IN)

33 CM (13 IN)

Position the batch on benchtop, such that 'open ends' of the letter facing towards you and ay from you.

2 Roll out the pastry away from you and towards you until it is at least 35 cm (13¾ in) deep. Now, working side to side, roll your pastry out, to a width of at least 24 cm/9½ in (this will yield six danish, with some trim).

3 Using a ruler and a paring knife, mark out and cut your pastry to a rectangle of 33 cm (8½ in) deep by 22 (13 in) cm wide. Reserve any trim for cruffins or scrap pastry.

4 As per the image abo mark and cut six squares, each measuring 11 × 11 cm (4½ x 4½ in). Using a shar knife, cut incisions in the left and bottom right corr of each square, ensuring the top right and bottom corners remain uncut.

APING

Position one square on bench, such that the ions are in the top left bottom right corners.

2 Gently lift the bottom right corner of the pastry and fold it over, to align with the incision in the top left corner. Using your fingertips gently press the pastry down to secure it.

3 Ever so slightly stretch out the thin strip of pastry in the top left corner, creating a little extra length.

4 Fold the top left corner of pastry over to the new bottom right corner, alignir the edges of pastry so that the new folded strip sits flush on top of the base. Using your fingertips, gentl press the pastry down to secure it.

ange the six shaped danishes on a baking tray lined with baking paper, ensuring that ther mple space between each pastry to allow for proving and baking. Reserve in the fridge

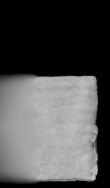

the batch on
p, such that the
of the letter are
rds you
om you.

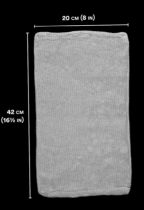

20 cm (8 in)

42 cm (16½ in)

2 Roll out the pastry away from you and towards you until it is at least 42 cm (16½ in) deep. Now, working side to side, roll your pastry out, to a width of at least 20 cm (8 in).

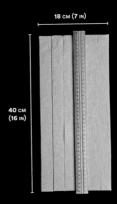

18 cm (7 in)

40 cm (16 in)

3 Using a ruler and a paring knife, mark out and cut your pastry to a rectangle measuring 40 cm (16 in) deep by 18 cm (7 in) wide.

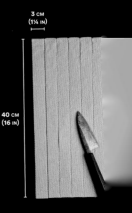

3 cm (1¼ in)

40 cm (16 in)

4 As per the image mark and cut the rect in six strips of pastry measuring 40 cm (16 long and 3 cm (1¼ in)

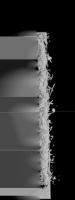

our filling of
y along the
 strip of
ng about
 of the strip
u uncovered.

2 Starting from the end furthest from you, roll up the strip of pastry, not too tightly (you don't want to lose your filling!)

3 Flip the rolled past onto one of its flat side such that the spiral is facing up.

greased and lined springform tins (ring only) on a lined baking tray. Position eac
argot in the centre of a prepared springform ring, to ensure that it will prove an

Torsade

CUTTING

26 CM (10 IN)

27 CM (10½ IN)

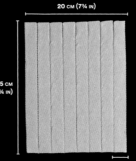

20 CM (7¾ IN)

25 CM (9¾ IN)

2.5 CM (1 IN)

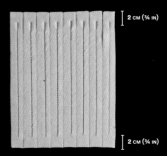

2 CM (¾ IN)

2 CM (¾ IN)

1 Position the batch on the benchtop, such that the 'open ends' of the letter are facing towards you and away from you.

2 Roll out the pastry away from you and toward you until it is at least 27 cm (10½ in) deep. Now, working side to side, roll your pastry out, to a width of at least 26 cm (10 in).

3 Using a ruler and a paring knife, mark out and cut your pastry, such that you have a rectangle measuring 25 cm (9¾ in) deep by 20 cm (7¾ in) wide.

Now cut this rectangle into eight strips of pastry measuring 25 cm (9¾ in) long by 2.5 cm (1 in) wide.

4 Using your ruler, carefully cut a slit down the middle of each strip of pastry, leaving 2 cm (¾ in) of pastry un-cut at each end of the strips.

SHAPING

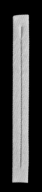

1 Open the slit such the pastry makes a loose diamond shape on the benchtop.

2 Take the bottom of the strip of pastry (the end closest to you), and bring it under itself, through the loop and back towards you. Repeat this step once.

3 Now take the top of the strip of pastry (the end furthest from you), and bring it over the top of itself, through the loop, and away from you. Again, repeat this step once. You should now have four twists in your torsade.

4 Check the even distribution of your twists; working carefully, you can slightly manipulate them.

Place on a baking tray lined with baking paper, ensuring that the torsades are evenly spaced, to allow for proving and baking. Reserve in the fridge until ready to prove. Carefully cover the tray with cling film to avoid a dry skin forming.

Cruffin

Originally the cruffin was born out of a way to use up pastry trim, and as such, it is the most forgiving of the pastry styles, based more on weight of the raw pastry rather than exact dimensions.

A cruffin is made from two strips of pastry, each weighing approximately 40 g (1½ oz). If you are a stickler for detail, the *ideal* dimensions of one strip is about 25 cm (9¾ in) long and 2.5 cm (1 in) wide. While all the different shape batches yield a cruffin or two from their leftover trim, you may well want to use an *entire* batch of pastry to make eight cruffins.

It is important to ensure that for a cruffin, both sides of the strip of pastry have cut edges to expose the lamination. If you use pastry from the very edge of your batch, you will have doughy, tight and ultimately, heavy cruffins that don't achieve lightness through separation of layers in the baking process.

I've included the proving and baking of cruffins in this chapter, as essentially the cruffin recipe remains the same up until post-bake, when the fillings and garnishes are applied.

PROVING

1   Place the loose-based dessert pan full of cruffins in the middle of a tray lined with baking paper. Now cover the cruffin tin loosely with a piece of baking paper and place a clean baking tray on top – the purpose of this is the control the way the cruffins prove, keeping their shape uniform.

2   Place your tray of cruffins in your turned-off oven with a dish of boiling water in the bottom, allow to prove for 5–6 hours. The cruffins are ready to bake when they protrude out of the holes of the dessert pan by about 1 cm (½ in), and have a flat top created by the tray weighting them down. The cruffins have overproven if the muffin 'tops' have started to grow sideways and are touching each other.

BAKING

1   Remove the proven cruffins from your oven then preheat to 210°C fan (410°F).

2   Carefully remove the baking paper from the top of the cruffins. Starting at the two corners closest to you, begin peeling very, very slowly, a centimetre at a time. I would even recommend getting down to eye level and working to ensure that you don't tear or pull any of the layers. The paper may be wet and harder to remove as a result of the humidity in the proving phase. Patience is key for this step!

3   Beat one egg to make the egg wash, then gently, following the same circular pattern as the shape of the top of the cruffins, using a soft bristled pastry brush, egg-wash the tops of the cruffins. Load into the preheated oven and bake at 210°C fan (410°F) for 5 minutes.

4   After the first 5 minutes of baking, knock the oven back to 160°C fan (320°F) and bake for a further 15 minutes. After this phase, open your oven and spin the tray 180 degrees and bake for a final 6 minutes, until the tops are a deep golden brown.

5   The cruffins are fully baked when you can carefully spin one in its tin.

6   Once baked, rest the cruffins for 5 minutes in their tins, then remove from the tins and cool on a wire baking rack.

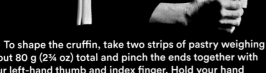

1 To shape the cruffin, take two strips of pastry weighing about 80 g (2¾ oz) total and pinch the ends together with your left-hand thumb and index finger. Hold your hand upright so that the length of the two pieces drape over the top of your index finger.

2 Take the inside cruffin piece and bring it up and over your thumbnail so the piece is now on the outside – you will see the centre of a spiral forming.

3 Take the other strip, which will now be on the inside, and bring it up and over the previous piece.

4 Repeat this motion until you have about 3 cm (1¼ in) of pastry left of each strip – forming two 'tails' of equal length.

5 If you have rolled the cruffin correctly, these 'tails' of pastry should be directly opposite each other.

6 Gently removing your left-hand thumb and forefinger, turn the partially shaped cruffin over to be flat in the palm of your left hand, exposing the underside where the tails are.

7 Fold each overhanging tail back in towards the opposite side. The whole process should be done maintaining tension while shaping the pastry without actually stretching it.

Place the shaped cruffins into greased and lined cups of the dessert pan (or muffin tin), ensuring the spiral side is facing up and the tucked 'tails' of the pastry are on the underside.

Breakfast

Ousia

Mary was the first person to ever entrust me professionally with her KitchenAid. Now, owning a bakery myself, I have a true understanding of the level of faith required to hire someone with an Aerospace Engineering degree and zero experience in any form of commercial food preparation.

I was a regular coffee drinker at her tiny, yet perfect café, Ousia. One morning, sipping my flat white, I worked up the courage to ask Mary if she would hire me to do the daily baking for her café. Much to my shock, she agreed, and just like that, I was suddenly someone who got to bake for a living.

They should make a movie about Mary and Ousia. You couldn't help but be totally starstruck by her. Not only was she arrestingly beautiful, she had a way of making you feel incredibly special (and she somehow had the capacity to extend that divine gift to everyone who crossed the threshold of her little Ousia). But mostly, the food she prepared was mind-blowingly delicious, visually stunning, soulful, medicinal, a culinary trip around the Mediterranean, and every single dish was made with love. You could taste it. Mary would spend her days off combing the markets for the best of the in-season fruits and vegetables, then return to the kitchen and create magical dishes, respecting traditional recipes and methods.

Mary taught me to love food. Not just the enjoyment in the eating, but the pleasure in the preparation; respect for ingredients and their transformation into something so much more than the sum of their parts.

On and off, for two years, I worked for Mary and her gorgeous husband, Alec, and I slowly built up my knowledge of baking, and my confidence in a kitchen. During this time, I started to develop a fascination for more complex patisserie. One day upon returning home from work, I received delivery of a book that I'd ordered on Paris patisseries. Sitting crossed legged on the living room floor I randomly opened the beautiful coffee table book. The double page spread that beheld me portrayed a stack of pains au chocolat, photographed so closely that you could appreciate every perfect, individual layer of pastry. It was one of the most beautiful photos I had ever seen.

Practically hypnotised, I closed the book, took myself to the nearest travel agent, and booked a ticket to Paris.

At Ousia the following morning I excitedly relayed my story of the book, the photo, and the subsequent ticket to Paris. After a little back-and-forth, Mary and Alec decided they would join me.

Traditional Croissant

YIELDS 5–8

1 batch of pastry, rolled out
and cut for croissants

1 egg, beaten ('egg wash')

Arguably the most ubiquitous of all breakfast pastries, the croissant has been gracing morning kitchen tables for the last couple of hundred years in its current format, but its credited predecessor, the Austrian *kipferl*, dates all the way back to the 1300s. Safe to say, this is a pastry that has stood the test of time.

The croissant's legendary buttery taste and flaky consistency, with a delicate crunch on the outside, and soft folds of impossibly thin honeycomb-like dough on the inside, equally lends itself to being eaten fresh, straight from the bag as you exit a bakery, slathered with your favourite preserve, or filled with ham and cheese. Croissants are the foundational product of Lune, and the pastry that made me fall head-over-heels in love with baking.

Croissants take 5–6 hours to prove. If you want to eat fresh croissants for breakfast (let's say 8am), here is where it's going to get very real …

SHAPING SEE PAGE 32

PROVING

1   Set your alarm for 2am, get out of bed and put the kettle on. Take your tray of croissants out of the fridge, remove the cling film (plastic wrap), then transfer them them to your oven. Do NOT turn the oven on. You are simply using your oven to simulate a proving cabinet. Once the kettle is boiled, fill your favourite baking dish (I use my lasagne dish) with 2.5 cm (1 in) of boiling water. Place this dish in the very bottom of your oven, close the door, and go back to bed. Welcome to the life of a baker.

2   The ideal environment for proving the croissants is 25°C (77°F) with a high level of humidity, but unless you have a commercial prover in your kitchen, you're not going to be able to control this exactly. At 25°C (77°F) the croissants take about 6 hours to prove. If you live in a warm climate, your croissants will prove quicker, if the standard room temperature in your house is typically cooler than 25°C (77°F), they may take a little longer. It's not prescriptive, so assess how the croissants look when you wake up, and if they look like they need a little more time, be patient and give them a little longer. →

BAKING

1 Once you have decided that the croissants are ready to bake (see note), remove the tray of proven croissants from the oven, as well as the baking dish with water. Pre-heat your oven to 210°C fan (410°F).

2 Using a pastry brush with soft bristles, carefully apply the egg wash, ensuring you don't use so much that it pools at the base of the croissants.

3 Bake the croissants for 5 minutes at 210°C fan (410°F), then knock your oven back to 160°C fan (320°F) and bake for a further 16 minutes. If you know your oven well and it has a hot spot, rotate your tray 180 degrees for the last 8 minutes.

4 When they are ready, they should be an even golden colour all over.

5 Although tempting (because your kitchen will smell absolutely amazing) resist biting into one straight from the oven. Apart from the fact that the steam inside them will be searing hot and almost certainly burn you, they need at least 10–15 minutes after coming out of the oven to continue cooking, using the residual heat inside the shell to finish baking the inner layers.

Congratulations! You've just successfully made croissants at home. Now, bon appétit!

CHEF NOTE I have an odd way of explaining to new pastry chefs at Lune what a perfectly proven croissant looks like. To me, it looks something similar to the skin of a beach volleyballer. Perfectly smooth, no cellulite, not sinewy. It's totally filled out its skin and is tight and flawless. It will almost look cartoon-like and will have more than doubled in size.

Ham and Gruyère Croissant

YIELDS 5

1 batch of pastry, rolled out and cut for croissants

seeded mustard, to taste

100 g (3½ oz) shaved double smoked leg ham

75 g (2½ oz) Gruyère, finely grated, plus extra to garnish

1 egg, beaten ('egg wash')

This is no café counter ham and cheese croissant. You know the ones; slightly sad looking, cut in half, and stuffed with ham and cheese, then forced to suffer the indignity of being squashed and toasted in a sandwich press … need I go on?

No, this is a LUNE ham and Gruyère croissant. We add the ham, cheese, and a sneaky dollop of vinegary seeded mustard *before* shaping the raw croissant. This means that it all bakes together in one glorious flaky, cheesy masterpiece. Some people love the crunchy ear of the croissant where the cheese has oozed out and formed a crispy layer over the pastry. Some love the string of Gruyère that stretches from the pastry to your lips, if you eat it still warm. There's definitely an argument for the best bit being not knowing where the cheese stops and the pastry starts; that tender, slightly doughy layer where the two marry (and live happily ever after). My favourite bit is the mustard, surprising and zingy, a little bit of acidity that cuts through the decadence of the butter and Gruyère.

If we ever took this off the menu at Lune there would be a riot of biblical proportions.

SHAPING

1   As per the traditional croissants, gently holding the wide base of the triangle in your left hand, confidently, but smoothly, stretch the dough by running your right thumb down the length of the triangle, aiming for a length of about 40 cm (16 in). Stretch out all five of the croissants on the benchtop.

2   At the wide end of one of the croissants, put a pea-sized dollop of the seeded mustard and, using a small offset palette knife, spread it a little. Now place 20 g (¾ oz) of shaved ham, fluffed up (not folded or squished into a tight ball) on top of the mustard. Finally, place 15 g (½ oz) of grated gruyère on top of the ham. Repeat for the remaining four croissants.

3   Starting from the wide end of the triangle, and using your thumbs to keep the ham and cheese in place, roll up the pastry, finishing with the tip of the triangle on the underside of the croissant, and the 'ears' of the croissant touching your benchtop (they will act as little scoops to contain any rebellious cheese that oozes out in the baking process). Repeat for the remaining four croissants.

4   Place the shaped ham and Gruyère croissants on a baking tray, well spaced to allow them to expand during the proving and baking process. If you are not going to begin proving them immediately, reserve in the fridge, loosely covering the tray with cling film to avoid a dry skin forming.   →

PROVING

1 Sorry team, when it comes to proving, just like the traditonal croissants the ham and Gruyère croissants also take 5–6 hours to prove (you're going to see a pattern developing here); so you will need to plan for that, based on when you want to eat them. (Tip: maybe have them for lunch so you don't have to get up in the middle of the night?!). Place your tray of shaped ham and gruyère croissants in your turned-off oven with a dish of boiling water in the bottom. Allow to prove for 5–6 hours, checking them from the 5-hour mark, to ensure they don't overprove.

BAKING

1 The ham and Gruyère croissants are ready to bake when they are puffy, filled out, the surface is smooth, and they have more than doubled in size.

2 Remove the tray of proven croissants and the dish of water from the oven. Preheat your oven to 210°C fan (410°F).

3 Using a soft-bristled pastry brush, carefully apply the egg wash, ensuring you don't use so much that it pools at the base of the croissant. Now sprinkle a small amount of the extra grated gruyère on top.

4 Bake the croissants for 5 minutes at 210°C fan (410°F), then knock your oven back to 160°C fan (320°F) and bake for a further 16 minutes. If you know your oven well and it has a hot spot, rotate your tray 180 degrees for the last 8 minutes.

5 Allow to cool for at least 10 minutes before having one of the greatest culinary moments of your life.

Cheese and Vegemite Escargot

YIELDS 6

6 springform tins (ring only), 11 cm (4½ in) in diameter, greased and lined with baking paper and placed on a lined baking tray

1 batch of pastry, rolled out and cut for escargot

Vegemite, to taste

200 g (7 oz) béchamel

150 g (5 oz) Gruyère, finely grated, plus extra for garnish

1 egg, beaten ('egg wash')

A pastry that will evoke childhood memories for any Australian kid, but also a sneaky sophisticated savoury offering, the Vegemite playing an important role in delivering a deep, rich umami quality to the flavour profile.

Don't worry, if you don't live in Australia and can't access Vegemite, any other spread made from yeast extract will work, such as Marmite or Promite.

BÉCHAMEL

20 g (¾ oz) butter

200 g (7 oz) milk

20 g (¾ oz) flour

¼ teaspoon seeded mustard

15 g (½ oz) Gruyère, grated

pinch of salt

1   Melt the butter in a small saucepan over a medium heat. In another saucepan, bring the milk and seeded mustard to a simmer, then remove immediately from the heat.

2   Add the flour to the melted butter and stir continuously with a whisk until fully combined – this is called a roux. Cook the roux over a medium heat until it just starts to catch on the bottom of the pan and becomes blonde in colour.

3   While continuing to whisk the roux, begin to pour in the warmed milk. Once all the milk is added, bring the béchamel to a gentle boil and allow to boil for 1 minute, stirring continuously. Take off the heat and add the gruyère, stirring until the cheese has melted and fully combined. Finally, add the salt. Allow to cool to room temperature. If you're not going to use it immediately, transfer to sealed container and refrigerate.

SHAPING

1   You should have six strips of pastry measuring 40 cm (16 in) long by 3 cm (1¼ in) wide in front of you on the benchtop.

2   Using a small palette knife, spread a layer of Vegemite along the length of each strip of pastry, leaving about 3 cm (1¼ in) of pastry Vegemite free at the end of the strip. Depending on how much you love your Vegemite, you can be as scant or as generous as you want, remembering that one escargot is equivalent to a piece of toast (from a Vegemite quantity perspective!).

3   Apply 30 g (1 oz) of béchamel to each strip of pastry, and using an offset palette knife, spread evenly along the length, again leaving the last 3 cm (1¼ in) of pastry uncovered. (You can take the béchamel straight from the container it has been stored in, or you can transfer it into a piping bag, then pipe a thick seam of the béchamel along the length of the pastry.)

4   Sprinkle 25 g (1 oz) of grated Gruyère along the length of each strip, covering the béchamel as evenly as possible.

5   Starting from the end furthest from you, roll up each strip one at a time, not too tightly. Place each rolled escargot in a greased, lined springform ring, ensuring that it is in the centre of each ring so it proves and bakes evenly. →

PROVING

1 As per the traditional croissant, the cheese and Vegemite escargot takes 5–6 hours to prove, so once again, plan backwards based on when you want to bake and eat them. Place your tray of cheese and Vegemite escargots in your turned-off oven with a dish of boiling water in the bottom and allow to prove for 5–6 hours. They are ready when they are touching the sides of the springform ring.

BAKING

1 Remove the proven escargots and dish of water from your oven, then heat it to 210°C fan (410°F).

2 The escargot is one of the only pastries where you will have permission to egg-wash indelicately. You almost want to be a *little* bit 'rough'. Press very firmly on the top of the proven pastry with the flat of the pastry brush, drenched with egg wash. Think of it as 'gluing the layers of the escargot together' – this will help prevent the centre spiralling out. Finally, sprinkle each escargot with 10 g (⅓ oz) of extra grated Gruyère.

3 Bake the escargots for 5 minutes at 210°C fan (410°F) then knock your oven back to 160°C fan (320°F) and bake for a further 16–20 minutes, looking for an even colour to indicate that they are finished baking. Rotate the tray 180 degrees in the final few minutes if you know your oven has a hot spot.

4 When you are happy with the colour, remove from oven and, using oven mitts, carefully remove the springform ring and allow to cool. Resist for at least 10 minutes before serving!

Kouign-Amann

YIELDS 6

6 springform tins,
11 cm (4½ in) in diameter

100 g (3½ oz) softened butter
(to mayonnaise consistency,
so it's spreadable but not
totally melted)

caster (superfine) sugar,
for the tins

sea salt flakes

1 batch of pastry, rolled out and
cut for kouign-amann (escargot)

I discovered the kouign-amann when I was living in Paris and staging at Du Pain et des Idées. Every Saturday morning, I would drop off my washing at a laundrette then go to the nearest patisserie for breakfast. On one particular occasion, I noticed an escargot-esque pastry in the display counter. It wasn't a 'pain au raisin' because it didn't appear to have any filling swirled through it. Simply put, it was a large spiral-shaped hockey puck of immense golden layered beauty, and I wanted to eat it. But due to its somewhat intimidating name, it took me a while to build up the courage to order it.

I'm not going to beat around the bush: when I finally did, it was one of the best things I'd ever eaten. Sweet, salty, caramelised (to the point *just* before bitter), crunchy, chewy … pretty much everything you could ever want in a pastry. The kouign-amann has been on the menu at Lune since 2013, and is a firm customer and staff favourite, affectionately nicknamed the KA. If you know, you know …

The best thing about the kouign-amann is that it does not rely on perfect lamination for an amazing result. In fact, originally the Brittany-based pastry was made with leftover bread dough, laminated with butter and sugar, to produce a dessert.

TIN PREPARATION

1   Brush the springform tins with a liberal amount of softened butter, then tip a tablespoon of sugar in each tin and toss around to coat the base and sides evenly. The quantity of sugar isn't too important, as you will tip out any excess sugar that doesn't stick to the buttered tins. Keep excess sugar for shaping the kouign-amann later. Finally, sprinkle a large pinch of sea salt flakes over the base of each tin.

SHAPING

1   Brush the remaining softened butter (you should have at least 50 g/1¾ oz left over from the tin preparation) evenly along the length of the six strips of pastry. Now sprinkle an even blanket of sugar over the butter, leaving the last 3 cm (1¼ in) of each strip unsugared. The amount of sugar isn't prescriptive, as it's difficult to be accurate. You want to make sure the butter is totally covered, but the sugar isn't thick. If there are areas that the sugar looks thicker, use your index finger to gently spread the sugar evenly.

2   Roll the first strip gently towards you, creating little to no tension as you go. Now carefully pick up the tight spiral and dip both the top and bottom surfaces (the spiral faces) in the reserved sugar, then place in the centre of a prepared tin. Repeat for the remaining strips of pastry.

3   Arrange the tins with the shaped kouign-amann on a baking tray lined with baking paper and reserve in the fridge until you are ready to begin proving. →

PROVING	1 Place your tray of KAs in your turned-off oven with a dish of boiling water in the bottom and allow to prove for 5–6 hours. They are ready when they are at least doubled in size, and touching the sides of the tin. The sugar will appear wet.

| **BAKING** | 1   Remove the tray of proven KAs and the dish of water from your oven, then heat it to 210°C fan (410°F). While your oven is warming up, chill the KAs in the fridge; this will help them to hold their shape during baking.

2   Once your oven is at temperature, remove the tray of KAs from the fridge and load immediately into the oven. Bake for 5 minutes at 210°C fan (410°F), then knock your oven back to 160°C fan (320°F) and bake for a further 5 minutes. During this time, prepare a second baking tray with baking paper and set it on your benchtop next to a heatproof cooling rack.

3   At this 10-minute mark, remove your KAs from the oven, set the tray down on the heatproof cooling rack and, using oven mitts, very carefully pick up each tin and flip it upside-down onto the clean baking tray, lifting the empty tin carefully off the flipped pastry so as not to damage any of the outer layers that may be inclined to stick to the tin. The pastry is underbaked at this point, and the sugar is molten, so proceed with extreme caution. Using an offset palette knife, carefully transfer each flipped KA back into the tins.

4   Place the tray of flipped KAs back into the oven at 160°C fan (320°F) for a further 10–12 minutes. They are ready when they have achieved a deep golden colour that is only ever so slightly paler in the centre.

5   Once removed from the oven, as quickly as is safe to do so, use oven mitts to turn the finished pastries out of their tins and onto the second baking tray lined with new baking paper, ensuring that they are not touching each other; as the sugar cools it will harden and they will stick steadfastly to each other. |
|---|---|

The kouign-amann is one of the rare pastries at Lune with an agreeably long shelf life. I would not recommend eating them 10 minutes after they are out of the oven – instead, give them a good length of time to cool completely, for a crispy and chewy experience, all in one.

Pain Au Chocolat

YIELDS 6

1 batch of pastry, rolled out
and cut for pain au chocolat

12 chocolate batons,
about 10 g (⅓ oz) each

1 egg, beaten ('egg wash')

Since leaving Formula One behind for the buttery world of croissants, almost every single Frenchman I've crossed paths with has the same reaction when I mention my new area of expertise. Instantly transported back to their childhoods, their eyes glaze over with blissful memories of 'Le Goûter', or afternoon tea, as we know it. It seems that the archetypal pain au chocolat is a popular favourite *goûter* for many French children. It's always a lovely reminder to me of how food can trigger the most visceral of memories.

At Lune, we've found it's more common for the pain au chocolat to be enjoyed as a cheeky little breakfast treat (perhaps that's an Aussie thing), but no judgement here; whether it's breakfast, afternoon tea, or a midnight snack (Meryl Streep and Steve Martin style), you're in for a good time.

The pain au chocolat sits permanently on the menu at Lune, but it's also one of those *classics* that we've had a bit of fun with. Following this recipe are three Lune variations.

SHAPING SEE PAGE 34

PROVING

1   Place your tray of shaped pain au chocolat in your turned-off oven with a dish of boiling water in the bottom and allow to prove for 5–6 hours, checking them from the 5-hour mark, to ensure they don't overprove.

BAKING

1   A pain au chocolat is one of the most pleasing of all the proven pastries. When ready to bake they look like smooth, puffy little pillows with a matte surface. If you have achieved this, you've completely nailed your raw pastry recipes – well done! Remove the tray of proven pain au chocolat from the oven, as well as the dish of water, then heat your oven to 210°C fan (410°F).

2   Using a soft-bristled pastry brush, carefully apply the egg wash. I like to use long sweeping strokes along the top surface, from end to end. Do not egg-wash the ends of the pastry where the chocolate batons are visible.

3   Bake the pain au chocolat for 5 minutes at 210°C fan (410°F), then knock your oven back to 160°C fan (320°F) and bake for a further 16 minutes. If you know your oven well and it has a hot spot, rotate your tray 180 degrees for the last 8 minutes.

4   When they are ready, they should be an even golden colour all over.

This is one you want to eat fresh. Wait the obligatory 10–15 minutes, then bite into one, and experience next-level pastry enjoyment, as your chocolate will still be molten.

Pain Au Chocolat Variation
Choc Almond

1 batch of pastry, rolled out and cut for pain au chocolat

6 chocolate batons, about 10 g (⅓ oz) each

½ batch of Almond Frangipane (Essentials, see page 262)

1 egg, beaten ('egg wash')

flaked almonds

icing (powdered) sugar, for dusting

In the early days of Lune, there were never any leftover croissants at the end of each day (and almond croissants are traditionally made from day-old croissants!) However, such was the demand for an almond croissant, I came up with a hybrid pain au chocolat, incorporating a seam of almond frangipane through the centre, topped with flaked almonds and served dusted with icing (powdered) sugar.

It was an instant hit. Lighter than a classic almond croissant, it still delivered on the flavour profile and offered a hint of that slightly chewy, almost macaron-like texture.

SHAPING

1 Pipe a thick line of almond frangipane along the top edge of each rectangle. Place 1 chocolate baton on top of the frangipane then, picking up the top edge of the pastry, roll up towards you, ensuring (as per the pain au chocolat) that the join finishes on the underside of the rolled pastry.

PROVE AS PER PAIN AU CHOCOLAT SEE PAGE 59

BAKE AS PER PAIN AU CHOCOLAT WITH THE BELOW VARIATION SEE PAGE 59

1 After egg-washing the pastries, sprinkle flaked almonds over the top, before loading into the oven.

2 After baking, allow to cool for at least 10 minutes, then dust with icing (powdered) sugar and serve.

Pain Au Chocolat Variation

Choc Pistachio

YIELDS 6

1 batch of pastry, rolled out and cut for pain au chocolat

6 chocolate batons, about 10 g (⅓ oz) each

½ batch of Pistachio and Rosewater Frangipane (Essentials, see page 262)

1 egg, beaten ('egg wash')

chopped pistachios

icing (powdered) sugar, for dusting

Pistachio and chocolate is a popular viennoiserie flavour combination, more commonly represented in escargots. Don't worry, I can personally attest to this equally delicious pain au chocolat format!

SHAPE AS PER CHOC ALMOND SEE PAGE 60

PROVE AS PER PAIN AU CHOCOLAT SEE PAGE 59

BAKE AS PER PAIN AU CHOCOLAT WITH THE BELOW VARIATION SEE PAGE 59

50 g (1¾ oz) dark baking chocolate

1   After egg-washing the pastries, sprinkle chopped pistachios over the top, before loading into the oven.

2   After baking, allow to cool for at least 10 minutes, then dust with icing sugar. Finally, melt the dark chocolate in a heatproof bowl, transfer to a small disposable piping bag, and cut off only the very tip of the piping bag. While the chocolate is still warm and very much liquid, in a quick back-and-forth flick of the wrist, drizzle the melted chocolate over the top of the icing sugar-dusted pastries.

3   Wait for the chocolate to set, then serve.

Pain Au Chocolat Variation

Pain Au 'Reese'

YIELDS 6

1 batch of pastry, rolled out
and cut for pain au chocolat

½ batch of Peanut Butter
Frangipane (Essentials,
see page 262)

6 chocolate batons,
about 10 g (⅓ oz) each

½ batch of Salted Caramel
(Essentials, see page 264)

1 egg, beaten ('egg wash')

chopped salted peanuts

icing (powdered) sugar

50 g (1¾ oz) dark baking
chocolate

Whatever your frame of reference, chocolate, peanut and caramel is a guaranteed threesome made in heaven, and this Lune variation on the pain au chocolat is no exception.

SHAPING

1   Pipe a thick line of peanut butter frangipane along the top edge of each rectangle. Place one chocolate baton on top of the frangipane. Just in front of the frangipane, pipe a thin seam of salted caramel. Picking up the top edge of the pastry, roll up towards you, ensuring as per the pain au chocolat that the join finishes on the underside of the rolled pastry.

PROVE AS PER PAIN AU CHOCOLAT SEE PAGE 59

BAKE AS PER PAIN AU CHOCOLAT WITH THE BELOW VARIATION SEE PAGE 59

1   After egg-washing the pastries, sprinkle chopped peanuts over the top, before loading into the oven.

2   The baked pain au 'Reese' is dusted with icing (powdered) sugar and drizzled with chocolate. Feel free to channel your inner Jackson Pollock and get a bit wild and creative with your chocolate drizzling!

Morning Tea

As it happened, the fateful day in Paris was the seventh. Wandering the beautiful streets solo, I set myself a mission to visit the boulangerie where the trip-inspiring photo had been taken; Du Pain et des Idées, a beautiful restored boulangerie situated in the 10th arrondissement.

Entering the shop was what I can only describe as a blissful assault on the senses. The scent of butter and toasty flour already hits you halfway down Rue Yves Toudic, but the air inside the boulangerie, thick with butter, was nothing short of transcendental. Levels of anticipation rising, my eyes, spoilt for choice, didn't know what to take in first. But they settled upon the pains au chocolat. There they were, in all their three-dimensional glory, not just a depiction of architectural pastry perfection, but real-life flaky, golden layers, smugly ganged up together, just waiting to induce eye-rolling pleasure. Casting my eyes to the left and right I then took in the croissants, stacked artfully on cooling racks. Platters of different varieties of escargot, deeply golden chausson aux pommes, and then huge (HUGE) slabs of bread, thickly crusted, sold by weight and not loaf.

After an unknown period of time, I came out of my hypnotic state, only to discover that la vendeuse (the saleswoman) was laughing at me. Clumsily attempting to explain my story of how I came to be stood in her shop, she presently ducked out the back and returned with a gentleman, who she introduced as the owner and founder, Christophe Vasseur. Christophe had spent some time in Australia and spoke beautiful English. He very kindly humoured me while I prattled on about his extraordinary boulangerie, and sent me away with several pastries. On the steps of Montmartre, overlooking Paris, I savoured morsels of each pastry. Sitting there, I couldn't possibly have imagined the metamorphic significance of this moment.

The following day, in a small hotel in South Western France, I emailed Christophe to thank him for the beautiful pastries. Again, I dared to ask. Would Christophe consider hiring me, for an apprenticeship, even a stage (an unpaid internship)? The answer came back quickly.

'Yes, for someone like you (passionate and motivated), it is possible.'

Lemon Curd Cruffin

6–8 shaped and baked cruffins

200 g (7 oz) lemon sugar

300 g (10½ oz) lemon curd

candied lemon zest, to garnish

I elaborate on the history of the cruffin in the Afternoon Tea chapter, but all you really need to know for now is that the lemon curd cruffin is the most popular of all the cruffin flavours ever to grace the counter at Lune. The ideal morning treat, it combines lip smacking tartness from the lemon curd that perfectly offsets the richness of the beautiful buttery pastry.

The recipe for lemon curd makes more than you will need for this number of cruffins, but the curd keeps happily for a while, stored in sterilised jars in the fridge, so you may as well have a little extra on hand! When life gives you lemon curd …

All the following components should be prepared at least one day in advance.

LEMON CURD

200 g (7 oz) egg yolks

320 g (11¼ oz) caster (superfine) sugar

200 g (7 oz) lemon juice

grated zest of 2 lemons

320 g (11¼ oz) butter, at room temperature, cut into cubes

1   Fill a medium saucepan about one-third full of water. Bring to the boil, then reduce to a simmer. Meanwhile, whisk the egg yolks and sugar in a medium heatproof bowl. Add the lemon juice and zest and whisk to combine. Finally, add the cubes of butter. Place the heatproof bowl over the saucepan of simmering water (known as a *bain marie* or double boiler) to cook the curd, making sure that the bottom of the bowl isn't actually touching the water. Stir frequently, scraping down sides of the bowl and whisking the mixture at the bottom of the bowl to ensure that the eggs don't scramble.

2   Cool completely, then transfer 300 g (10½ oz) to a small disposable piping bag, and the rest into sterilised jars. Store in the fridge.

LEMON SUGAR

2 lemons

200 g (7 oz) caster (superfine) sugar, plus a little extra

1   Using a fine microplane, zest the lemons, completely removing all the rind. Rub the lemon zest into the 200 g (7 oz) of sugar with your fingers in a bowl, releasing the oil from the lemon. Allow the sugar to infuse with the zest.

2   When you are ready to finish the cruffins, pass the sugar through a sieve. It will feel a little clumpy and wet. Add small amounts of extra caster sugar to loosen the lemon-infused sugar, until you reach a consistency closely resembling the pure sugar.

CANDIED LEMON ZEST

4 lemons

250 g (9 oz) water

250 g (9 oz) caster (superfine) sugar

1   Using a citrus zester (not a microplane), remove the peel from the lemon in long, thin strips.

2   Make a simple syrup by combining the water and sugar in a saucepan and bringing to the boil, stirring to dissolve the sugar. Add the lemon zest to the boiling sugar syrup, reduce heat to barely a simmer, then put a lid on the saucepan and cook for 15 minutes until the zest is soft and completely sweet. If it is still bitter, or a bit toothsome, continue to cook, testing a piece of zest every 15 minutes. Store candied lemon zest in its cooking syrup in the fridge.

3   Refrigerate the candied lemon zest and syrup in a sealed container.   →

ASSEMBLING

1 Ensure that the cruffins have been out of the oven for at least 5 minutes, removed from their tins, and are cooling on a wire rack.

2 Next, you will need to to coat them in the lemon-infused sugar. This should be done while the cruffins are still warm (approximately 5 minutes after being removed from their tins), otherwise the sugar will not stick to the pastry. Have your sugar in a medium bowl and, one at a time, gently toss each cruffin in the lemon sugar, turning it to make sure you achieve full sugar coverage, then shake off any excess. After each one has been tossed in the lemon sugar, return it to the wire rack. Cool for 20 minutes before proceeding.

3 Now, with a small paring knife, make a vertical incision in the middle of the top of the cruffin, making sure not to cut all the way through. This incision will allow you to poke the piping bag into the cruffin to fill it.

4 Using your digital kitchen scales, place one cruffin on the scales and 'tare' the scales to zero. Cut the tip off your piping bag, creating an opening of 3–4 mm. Now place the tip of the piping bag as deep as possible into the incision without damaging the top of the cruffin and squeeze the piping bag to fill the cruffin with lemon curd. Stop filling when your scales read 35–40 g (1¼–1½ oz).

5 You should finish with a little button of curd on top of the cruffin.

6 Finally, garnish the little button of curd with two to three strips of candied lemon zest.

Coconut Kouign-Amann

YIELDS 6

6 springform tins, 11 cm (4½ in) in diameter (prepare tins as per the Kouign-Amann recipe on page 55)

1 batch of pastry, rolled out, but mark and cut the batch only to the stage where you have 6 × 11 cm (4½ in) squares, do not make any internal incisions, as instructed for danishes (page 35)

300 g (10½ oz) coconut caramel

100 g (3½ oz) brown sugar syrup

raw sugar, for dipping

This Lune adaptation takes on the original form of the kouign-amann (unlike the spiral shape of Lune's Kouign-Amann, featured in the Breakfast chapter).

Inspiration for this pastry came from one of our talented pastry chefs who has a Filipino background. The pan de coco is a traditional Filipino treat; a sweetened white bread roll filled with sweetened grated coconut flesh.

For this adaptation of the kouign-amann, the addition of the coconut caramel amplifies the gratifying chewiness of the pastry, and the brown sugar adds a molassesy depth of bitter-sweetness.

COCONUT CARAMEL

110 g (3¾ oz) caster (superfine) sugar

75 g (2½ oz) coconut cream

45 g (1½ oz) butter

2 g salt

75 g (2½ oz) desiccated (shredded) coconut

1   Place a small, clean saucepan over a medium heat. Once the pan is hot, gradually sprinkle in some of your sugar, wait for it to melt, then sprinkle in a little more, waiting each time until all the sugar is melted before adding more. Once the sugar is melted and evenly caramelised, reaching a deep brown consistency, remove from the heat and slowly pour in the coconut cream, whisking continuously. Once all the coconut cream is in, add the butter and salt and whisk to fully combine. Finally stir in the desiccated coconut.

2   Once cooled, transfer to a piping bag. The coconut caramel can be made ahead and stored in the fridge until required.

BROWN SUGAR SYRUP

200 g (7 oz) brown sugar

100 g (3½ oz) water

1   Combine both ingredients in a saucepan and bring to the boil, stirring continuously to ensure the sugar fully dissolves. Once the syrup has reached a rolling boil, remove from the heat, allow to cool completely, then transfer to a container and store in the fridge until required. If you have a squeezy bottle, you can also transfer the cooled syrup directly into this; it will make it easier to use in its application for this recipe.

SHAPING

1   Cut a 4 mm opening in the tip of the piping bag of coconut caramel, then pipe a diamond of coconut caramel on the square of pastry, the points of the diamond occurring at the centre point of each side of the pastry square. Now fill in the diamond with caramel. Repeat this for all 6 squares of pastry.

2   Carefully fold each corner of the pastry into the centre, creating a little parcel that completely covers the caramel diamond. Dip both sides of the pastry parcel into a bowl of raw sugar, making sure to get good coverage. Finally, place the pastry, folded side down, in the centre of the prepared tins.

3   Arrange the tins with shaped pastries on a baking tray and reserve in the fridge until you are ready to start them proving. →

PROVING

1 Place your tray of coconut kouign-amann in your turned-off oven with a dish of boiling water in the bottom and allow to prove for 5–6 hours. They are ready when they are at least doubled in size, and touching the sides of the tin.

BAKING

1 Remove the tray of proven coconut kouign-amann and the dish of water from your oven, then heat it to 210°C fan (410°F).

2 Taking your squeezy bottle of brown sugar syrup, squeeze a small amount of the syrup (about 15 g/½ oz) in a gap between the pastry and the tin.

3 Follow the same baking process as for the Kouign-Amann on page 55.

As per the Kouign-Amann, this pastry will improve with a decent resting and cooling period. One of the great joys of eating this pastry is the textural variation achieved as the caramels and sugars cool and harden, creating a toffee. So don't hoe into it immediately, because it is one of the rare viennoiseries that gets BETTER with time!

Pecan Sticky Bun

6 springform tins, 11 cm (4½ in) in diameter, greased and lined with baking paper

1 batch of pastry, rolled out and cut for escargot

300 g (10½ oz) butterscotch sauce

120 g (4¼ oz) pecan halves, roasted

100 g (3½ oz) pecan meal, roasted

200 g (7 oz) brown butter

200 g (7 oz) cinnamon sugar

1 egg, beaten ('egg wash')

What is a baking cookbook without a recipe for sticky buns? That may remain one of the great unanswered questions of our time, because I'm certainly not willing to be the first to go down that dark and perilous path.

At Lune we bake pecan sticky buns in individual tins (because we like to be different). Universally, however, a batch of sticky buns will be proved and baked in one large, deep tray.

If you don't have access to individual tins, you can absolutely proceed with this recipe using a high-sided tray or baking dish, approximately 30 × 20 cm (12 × 8 in). Prepare the tray as per the instructions for individual tins, and be sure to evenly arrange the shaped sticky buns in the tray, as you want them to uniformly prove and bake into each other. You will need to increase the baking time by 10–15 minutes to ensure that the buns bake all the way through.

BUTTERSCOTCH SAUCE

4 g vanilla

135 g (4¾ oz) maple syrup

45 g (1½ oz) brown sugar

180 g (6⅓ oz) butter

135 g (4¾ oz) cream

pinch of sea salt

PREPARE AHEAD OF TIME

1   Heat the vanilla, maple syrup, brown sugar, butter, and salt in a saucepan, whisking until the mixture is pulling away from the sides of the pan and thickly coating the back of a spoon. Finally, add the cream and whisk to fully emulsify. Allow to cool completely before transferring to piping bags.

2   The butterscotch sauce should be made ahead of time and kept refrigerated until required.

BROWN BUTTER

200 g (7 oz) butter

PREPARE AHEAD OF TIME

1   Prepare an ice bath. You will need two bowls, one slightly larger. Fill the larger bowl with ice and rest the smaller bowl inside the larger bowl, on top of the ice.

2   Meanwhile, melt the butter in a small saucepan over a medium heat, stirring frequently until fragrant and very dark. This is going to require a bit of bravery and trust in the classic French chefs that paved the way for our usage of brown butter in cooking! Be bold – you want to take it further than you think!

3   Remove from the heat and pour the browned butter into the bowl sitting on the ice bath. Continue to stir. Once the butter has stopped cooking and cooled slightly, but is still liquid, strain into a container using a sieve and refrigerate until required.

CINNAMON SUGAR

200 g (7 oz) caster (superfine) sugar

200 g (7 oz) brown sugar

2 g (about 1 teaspoon) cinnamon

1   Combine all the ingredients and whisk well to evenly distribute the cinnamon. This is more cinnamon sugar than you need for this recipe, but it will keep well, stored in an airtight container. →

SHAPING

1   Cover the base of each greased and lined springform tin with 40 g (1½ oz) of cooled butterscotch sauce – it is important that your butterscotch has firmed up and is more of a paste-like consistency for this step.

2   Scatter 20 g (¾ oz) of roasted pecan pieces on top of the butterscotch sauce in each tin. You can leave the pecan halves whole if you like, although I prefer them to be roughly chopped. Now sprinkle a teaspoon of the roasted pecan meal into the prepared tins.

3   Take the brown butter from the fridge, and, microwaving it in small bursts, 10 seconds at a time, gradually soften it to a thick mayonnaise consistency, stirring in between, taking care not to completely melt the butter.

4   Using a pastry brush, paint a thin and even layer of brown butter along each of the six strips of pastry, ensuring full coverage. Now sprinkle the cinnamon sugar evenly over the brown butter, leaving about 3 cm (1¼ in) at the bottom of each strip free from sugar. Finally, lightly cover the sugar with a thin layer of pecan meal, once again ensuring that the final 3 cm (1¼ in) remains uncovered.

5   Carefully roll one strip of pastry towards yourself, creating little to no tension as you go and finishing just before the point where the sugar and pecan meal stops. Now take the tail of the pastry and tuck it underneath the spiral you have just created. Place the rolled pastry, tucked tail side up, in the prepared tin and repeat with the remaining strips of pastry.

6   Once all the buns have been shaped, place the six tins on a baking tray and reserve in the fridge until you are ready to start them proving.

PROVING

1   Place your tray of shaped pecan sticky buns in your turned-off oven with a dish of boiling water in the bottom and allow to prove for 5–6 hours. The buns are ready to bake when they are touching the sides of the tin, about 2–3 times their original size. The sugar will also have melted slightly.

BAKING

1   Remove the tray of proven buns and the dish of water from the oven, then heat it to 210°C fan (410°F).

2   Egg wash each bun 'roughly', by pressing very firmly on the top of the tucked tail with the flat of the soaked pastry brush – you are essentially 'glueng it down'. This is not the presentation side, so don't worry too much about the direction of your brush strokes.

3   Bake the buns for 5 minutes at 210°C fan (410°F) then knock your oven back to 160°C fan (320°F) and bake for a further 16 minutes, again looking for an even colour to indicate that they are finished baking. Once again, rotate the tray 180 degrees in the final few minutes if you know your oven has a hot spot. The oven will smell strongly of caramel and nuts and you will see the butterscotch bubbling up the sides.

4   While the buns are in this phase of baking, prepare a wire rack on your benchtop with a clean baking tray lined with baking paper next to it.

5   Once your timer has gone off, remove the tray of buns from the oven and place it on the wire rack. Working quickly to avoid the caramel setting, using oven mitts, invert each sticky bun onto the clean tray in one swift 'flip and tap' movement. Leave the tins on the inverted pastries for 2 minutes to allow the nuts to set in place.

6   During this 2 minutes, melt your additional butterscotch sauce (either in a small saucepan over a medium heat, or in small bursts in a microwave, stirring between bursts) bringing it to a temperature where it is melted but not split.

7   Just before serving, drizzle the warm pecan sticky buns with the melted butterscotch sauce.

Danishes

At Lune we make two different styles of Danish. The more classic style is the baked danish, where the pastry is proven and then filled before baking. The second style, the blind-baked danish, was developed for one of the early Lune Lab desserts. We bake the danish with a square silicone insert, treating the danish as a baked tart shell and adding the fillings and garnishes after baking. This lends itself to fruits that are more delicious eaten fresh and uncooked.

Nappage is a glaze, classically prepared using apricot jam as the base. The jam is diluted with water to achieve a thinner consistency and any pieces of apricot are removed.

The following recipes give you three examples of each style, but really, once you've mastered the shaping, proving and baking of danishes, the flavour combinations are only limited by your imagination. Even with the recipes I've provided in this chapter, you can mix and match. For example, the quince and rhubarb are interchangeable and both work equally well with the supporting acts of custard and frangipane that sit beneath them.

SHAPING SEE PAGE 35

PROVING

1   Place your tray of shaped danishes in a turned-off oven with a dish of boiling water in the bottom and allow to prove for 4–5 hours. The danishes should at least double in size.

BAKING

1   Once your oven is at 210°C fan (410°F), load the prepared danishes into the oven. Bake at 210°C fan (410°F) for 5 minutes, then reduce the oven temperature to 160°C fan (320°F) and continue to bake for 12 minutes. Rotate the tray and bake for a final 4 minutes, to ensure even colour across all six danishes.

FINISHING

1   Apply the nappage as soon as the baked danishes are removed from the oven. Make sure your nappage is warm and a brushable liquid consistency. If you have made it in advance and stored it in the fridge, transfer it to a small saucepan and warm through, stirring with a spatula. You may need to add a little water to thin it out slightly. For baked danishes, nappage is applied over both the pastry and the fruit.

A danish eaten while still warm is one of life's great gifts. Treat yourself.

Baked Quince And Vanilla Danish

YIELDS 6

1 batch of pastry, rolled out
and cut for danish

poached quince

Vanilla Crème Pâtissière
(Essentials, see page 263)

1 egg, beaten ('egg wash')

Nappage
(Essentials, see page 265)

POACHED QUINCE

1 kg (2 lb 4 oz) water

800 g (1 lb 12 oz) white wine

1.2 kg (2 lb 10 oz) caster
(superfine) sugar

1 lemon, quartered

1 vanilla pod,
seeds already scraped

1 star anise

2–3 sprigs of thyme

2 quinces, peeled and quartered
(retain the peel and core)

PREPARE A DAY IN ADVANCE

1   In a large, deep saucepan, bring the water, wine and sugar to the boil, including the aromatics, quince peel and cores. Once the cooking syrup has reached the boil, add the quartered quinces, place a cartouche on top, reduce to barely a simmer, and cook for 4–6 hours. You will need to start testing how cooked the quinces are at the 4-hour mark, making sure they do not become too soft. Take off the heat when the quinces turn an orange colour.

2   Allow the quinces to cool in their cooking syrup overnight. They will continue to cook and darken in colour. The cooked quince quarters can be stored in a sealed container in their syrup in the fridge until required.

PREPARING THE PROVEN DANISHES FOR BAKING

1   Remove the tray of proven danishes and dish of water from the oven then preheat your oven to 210°C fan (410°F).

2   Prepare your quinces. Remove 6 quince quarters from their cooking syrup and place them on absorbent kitchen paper to soak up any excess syrup. Once they are not overly syrupy, transfer them carefully to a chopping board and cut them into slices approximately 3 mm thick, leaving the sliced quarters in place for now.

3   Pipe a thick layer of crème pâtissière inside the central square-shaped cavity of each danish. Slide a small offset palette knife under one of the sliced quarters of quince and gently, using your finger, press the quince quarter such that the slices fan out. Using the palette knife, carefully lift the fanned quince slices and place them on top of the crème pâtissière layer, gently tucking the quince slices underneath the pastry border if they happen to be wider than the cavity in the danish.

4   Finally, using a soft-bristled pastry brush, carefully egg-wash the borders and sides of the danish, brushing in the same direction as the lamination in the pastry, not across it.

BAKING AND FINISHING   SEE PAGE 83

Morning Tea

Rhubarb Bakewell Danish

YIELDS 6

1 batch of pastry, rolled out
and cut for danish

poached rhubarb

Almond Frangipane
(Essentials, see page 262)

1 egg, beaten ('egg wash')

Nappage
(Essentials, see page 265)

POACHED RHUBARB

250 g (9 oz) caster
(superfine) sugar

250 g (9 oz) water

lemon peel

1 bunch of rhubarb, leaves
removed, washed

1   Preheat your oven to 160°C fan (320°F).

2   Bring the sugar, water and lemon peel to the boil in a small saucepan over a medium heat, stirring to help the sugar dissolve evenly.

3   Meanwhile, using a ruler, cut one piece of rhubarb to a length of 6 cm (2½ in), then using this piece as a template, cut the rest of the rhubarb into 6 cm (2½ in) pieces. From each stalk you will have a piece left over that doesn't measure 6 cm (2½ in) – don't throw these out, I always still cook them, and have them on top of porridge (or ice cream ... let's be honest, nearly always ice cream).

4   Arrange the 6 cm (2½ in) pieces of rhubarb in one layer in a baking tray with a little bit of depth and pour the syrup over the rhubarb.

5   Cover the tray tightly with foil and place in the preheated oven. Rhubarb cooks surprisingly quickly – don't leave it unattended. You want it to be cooked, but still holding its shape. Remove the rhubarb from the oven after 10 minutes and test it by prodding it with a fork. If the rhubarb yields easily, it's ready, if there is still some resistance when you check it with the fork, replace the foil cover and return to the oven for another 5 minutes.

6   Once the rhubarb is cooked, transfer carefully to a shallow container and store in one layer, in its cooking syrup. Reserve in the fridge until required.

PREPARING THE PROVEN DANISHES FOR BAKING

1   Remove the tray of proven danishes and dish of water from the oven then preheat your oven to 210°C fan (410°F).

2   Prepare your rhubarb. Each danish will need 3–4 pieces of poached rhubarb. Remove up to 24 pieces of rhubarb from the container and place them on absorbent kitchen paper to soak up any excess syrup. I find that it helps to lay them out in groups of 3 or 4 pieces, based on their size, in preparation for placement in the danishes (you're aiming for a 6 × 6 cm/ 2½ in x 2½ in square of rhubarb pieces).

3   Pipe a layer of almond frangipane inside the central square-shaped cavity of each danish. Using an offset palette knife, carefully transfer 3–4 pieces of poached rhubarb and sit them neatly on top of the frangipane.

4   Finally, using a soft-bristled pastry brush, carefully egg-wash the borders and sides, brushing in the same direction as the lamination in the pastry, not across it.

Morning Tea

Baked Danish Variations

Chocolate Plum Sake Danish

YIELDS 6

1 batch of pastry, rolled out
and cut for danish

flourless chocolate cake

roasted plums

sake glaze

1 egg, beaten ('egg wash')

ROASTED PLUMS

4 plums, halved and
pits removed

100 g (3½ oz) brown sugar

50 g (1¾ oz) sake

1 star anise

1   Preheat your oven to 160°C fan (320°F).

2   Place the plums cut side down in a roasting tray. Sprinkle the brown sugar over the plums, then drizzle over the sake. Place the star anise in the tray. Roast the plums in the oven for 10 minutes, then test them: they need to be tender, but still holding together, remembering that they will be baked again in the danish. Once the plums are roasted to the desired consistency, store in a sealed container in the fridge in their roasting syrup.

3   Again, this recipe prepares slightly more plum than you will need for the six danishes. It allows for a couple of halves that may have cooked too much (or not enough). Basically, it's a delicious excuse to ensure there is some leftover plum!

FLOURLESS CHOCOLATE CAKE

100 g (3½ oz) butter

90 g (3¼ oz) dark cooking
chocolate

8 g (0.3 oz) cocoa powder

2 eggs, separated

110 g (3¾ oz) caster
(superfine) sugar

100 g (3½ oz) natural ground
almonds (almond meal)

1   Place the butter, dark chocolate and cocoa powder in saucepan over a low heat. Cook, stirring constantly, for 2–3 minutes or until melted and well combined. Remove from the heat and allow to cool slightly.

2   Meanwhile, beat the egg yolks and sugar in the bowl of a stand mixer fitted with the whisk attachment for 5 minutes, until thick and creamy. Transfer the whipped yolks and sugar to a mixing bowl, wash and dry the bowl of your stand mixer and the whisk attachment thoroughly, then beat the egg whites in the bowl of the stand mixer until soft peaks form.

3   Add the slightly cooled chocolate mixture and ground almonds to the beaten egg yolks and sugar, mixing with a spoon or spatula to combine. Finally, using a large metal spoon, gently fold half the egg whites into the chocolate mixture, being careful not to knock air out of the whites. Repeat with the remaining egg whites. Transfer carefully to a piping bag, and keep at room temperature until required. →

Morning Tea

CHEF NOTE You can use any variety of plum for this recipe. At Lune, our plum of choice was blood plum. This variation of a baked danish has its own unique sake glaze, replacing the nappage.

PREPARING THE PROVEN DANISHES FOR BAKING

1 Remove the tray of proven danishes and dish of water from the oven then preheat your oven to 210°C fan (410°F).

2 Prepare your plums. Each danish will have one plum half. Remove the best six plum halves from the container and place them on absorbent kitchen paper to soak up any excess syrup. Reserve the syrup that the plums were cooked in.

3 Pipe a 1 cm (½ in) layer of flourless chocolate cake batter inside the central square-shaped cavity of each danish. Using an offset palette knife, carefully transfer one plum half and place it cut side down on top of the chocolate cake mix.

4 Finally, using a soft-bristled pastry brush, carefully egg-wash the borders and sides of the danish, brushing in the same direction as the lamination in the pastry, not across it.

SAKE GLAZE
REPLACING NAPPAGE

plum syrup
(leftover from roasting)

sake

1 Bring the reserved plum syrup to a simmer in a small saucepan. Add a tablespoon of sake (or more, to suit your own taste). Allow to reduce slightly, to a glaze consistency.

BAKING AND FINISHING SEE PAGE 83

Blind-baked Danishes

6 cm (2½ in) square
silicone moulds

1 egg, beaten ('egg wash')

Blind-baked danishes have a slightly different baking and finishing process to the baked variety. All blind-baked danishes have the same initial process of baking the shell of the danish – the variations come with the different fillings, which are added post bake.

SHAPING SEE PAGE 35

PROVING SEE PAGE 83

BAKING

1   Remove the tray of proven danishes and dish of water from the oven and preheat the oven to 210°C fan (410°F).

2   Place a square silicone mould carefully in the centre of each danish, then half-fill each silicone insert with rice or baking beads. Now, using a soft-bristled pastry brush, carefully egg wash the borders and sides of the danish, brushing in the same direction as the lamination in the pastry, not across it.

3   Bake at 210°C fan (410°F) for 5 minutes, then reduce the oven temperature to 160°C fan (320°F) and continue to bake for 12 minutes. Rotate the tray and bake for a final 4 minutes, to ensure even colour across all six danishes.

4   Once out of the oven, carefully remove the silicone mould from each danish. Allow to cool completely.

Strawberry Miso Danish

YIELDS 6

6 danishes, blind baked
(as per instructions above)

miso crème diplomat

250 g (8¾ oz) strawberries,
hulled and thinly sliced

cracked black pepper

Nappage
(Essentials, see page 265)

BURNT MISO CARAMEL CUSTARD

75 g (2½ oz) miso paste

500 g (1 lb 2 oz) cream

200 g (7 oz) caster (superfine)
sugar, plus 25 g (1 oz) for
the custard

100 g (3½ oz) egg yolks

2 gelatine leaves, soaked

1   Preheat your oven to 150°C fan (300°F) and line a baking tray with baking paper. Spread the miso out in a thin, even layer and bake for 5–10 minutes, depending on quantity. You just want it to get a bit roasty, not burnt. Wait for it to start to get dark on top and caramelised around the edges. Remove from the oven and set aside to cool.

2   Pour the cream into a saucepan and bring to the boil, removing it from heat the instant it starts to boil.

3   Take a clean, dry saucepan, and put it over a medium heat. Once the pan is hot, gradually sprinkle in some of your sugar, wait for it to melt, then sprinkle in a little more, waiting each time until all the sugar is melted before adding more. Once the sugar is melted and evenly caramelised, reaching a deep brown consistency, remove from the heat and slowly pour in the hot cream, continuously whisking. Add the miso paste, whisk well to combine.

4   Meanwhile, whisk the egg yolks and the additional 25 g (1 oz) of sugar together in a bowl. Pour the warmed miso caramel into the egg mixture and whisk well to incorporate. Now transfer this back into the pan and whisk the mixture over medium heat until it begins to boil, and carry on whisking for about 3 minutes on the boil, until it reaches a nice thick consistency.

5   Remove from heat, add the soaked gelatine leaves and whisk until they are completely dissolved.

6   Transfer into either a tray or bowl, cover with cling film and leave to cool completely to room temperature then refrigerate overnight.

MISO CRÈME DIPLOMAT

200 g (7 oz) miso
caramel custard

100 g (3½ oz) double
(heavy) cream

Transfer the chilled custard into the bowl of a stand mixer fitted with a paddle attachment and beat on a low speed to gently loosen it. Carefully fold the cream through the custard, until it is just combined.

FINISHING

1   Evenly distribute the miso crème diplomat between the six danish shells, carefully spreading the custard to fill the corners. Alternatively, you can transfer the custard into a piping bag and pipe the custard into the shells.

2   For each danish, create a layer of overlapping thinly sliced pieces of strawberry that completely covers the crème diplomat.

3   Finally, brush the exposed pastry with warmed nappage, then season the strawberries with a little freshly cracked black pepper.

Mango Ginger Danish

YIELDS 6

6 danishes, blind baked
(as per instructions above)

Salted Caramel
(Essentials, see page 264)

ginger custard

50 g (1¾ oz) crystallised ginger,
finely diced

fresh mango slices,
approximately 2–3 mm thick

Nappage
(Essentials, see page 265)

GINGER CUSTARD

10 g (⅓ oz) fresh ginger, peeled

300 g (10½ oz) milk

½ vanilla pod, scraped

50 g (1¾ oz) caster
(superfine) sugar

4 egg yolks

10 g (⅓ oz) plain (all-purpose)
flour, sifted

10 g (⅓ oz) cornflour
(cornstarch), sifted

PREPARE A DAY IN ADVANCE

1   Using the flat of the blade of a chef's knife, crush the fresh ginger. Place the milk and crushed ginger in a saucepan and bring to the boil. Transfer the milk and ginger to a heatproof container, seal and store in the fridge overnight, to allow the milk to continue to infuse with the flavour of ginger.

2   The following day, strain the milk through a sieve back into a saucepan to remove the piece of crushed ginger, add the vanilla pod, then heat the milk and vanilla to just below boiling point, taking care to not allow a skin to form.

3   Meanwhile, whisk the caster (superfine) sugar with the egg yolks in a bowl until the mixture is pale and light. Whisk in the plain (all-purpose) flour and cornflour (cornstarch) and whisk well to combine.

4   When the milk is just about to boil, pour the milk gradually into the egg mixture, whisking constantly to incorporate. Now pour the egg and milk mixture back into the pan. Whisk the mixture continually over medium heat until it begins to boil, and carry on whisking for about 3 minutes on the boil, until the crème pâtissière reaches a nice thick consistency.

5   Take off the heat and pour into a clean bowl. Place cling film over the surface of the crème pâtissière to prevent a skin from forming, then store in the fridge until ready to use.

6   Just before you are ready to assemble the danishes, loosen the ginger infused custard with a hand whisk, then fold through the finely diced crystallised ginger.

FINISHING

1   Take your six cooled, unfilled blind-baked danish shells. Pipe a thin layer of salted caramel into the base of each danish (approximately 15 g/½ oz).

2   Loosen the ginger-infused custard with a hand whisk, then fold through the finely diced crystallised ginger. Evenly distribute the ginger custard between then six danish shells, carefully spreading the custard to fill the corners of the danish.

3   Carefully cover the ginger custard in each danish with the prepared slices of mango, layered on top of one another. This danish is a celebration of mango when they are at their best and juiciest in season, so make sure you don't skimp on the mango! Aim for at least 5 slices of mango cheek per danish.

4   Finally, brush the exposed edges of the pastry with warmed nappage.

Blind-baked Danish Variations
Blueberry Bay Danish

YIELDS 6

6 danishes, blind baked
(as per instructions above)

fromage blanc mousse

250 g (8¾ oz) blueberries

blueberry syrup

Nappage
(Essentials, see page 265)

FROMAGE BLANC MOUSSE

300 g (10½ oz) thickened cream

80 g (2¾ oz) egg yolks
(4 egg yolks)

130 g (4½ oz) caster (superfine) sugar

50 g (1¾ oz) water

2 gelatine leaves (gold strength), soaked

grated zest and juice of 1 lemon

250 g (9 oz) fromage blanc

PREPARE A DAY IN ADVANCE

1   Using a stand mixer fitted with the whisk attachment, whip the cream to stiff peaks. Once whipped, transfer the cream to another bowl and wash and dry the bowl and whisk attachment of the stand mixer thoroughly.

2   Again, using a stand mixer fitted with the whisk attachment, aerate the egg yolks. While the yolks are whisking, in a small saucepan bring the sugar and water to a rolling boil, stirring from the start to ensure that the sugar fully dissolves.

3   Slowly drizzle half the sugar syrup into the yolks while they are still being whisked.

4   Add the soaked gelatine leaves to the remaining sugar syrup and add into the whisking yolks. Continue whisking until the mixture is at room temperature (gauge this from the temperature of the bowl, it should not feel warm anymore).

5   Add the lemon juice and zest to the fromage blanc and, using a hand whisk, loosen the fromage blanc and ensure that the lemon juice is fully blended in.

6   In two stages, fold the whipped egg yolk mixture through the fromage blanc. Now fold the whipped cream into this mixture in two stages.

7   Transfer the mousse into a clean brownie tray, cover with a layer of baking paper or cling film to stop a skin from forming, and refrigerate overnight.

BLUEBERRY SYRUP

500 g (1 lb 2 oz) frozen blueberries

200 g (7 oz) caster (superfine) sugar

200 g (7 oz) water

10 fresh bay leaves

1   Place all the ingredients in a saucepan over a medium heat and stir to dissolve the sugar. Leaving the mixture over the heat, reduce until it is a thick and syrupy consistency. Allow to cool, then strain through a fine sieve. Reserve the strained liquid in a sealed container until required. Discard the blueberry pulp. →

FINISHING

1 Cut some of the blueberries in half, leaving the remaining whole. This variation in the blueberries not only increases the beauty of the finished pastry, but also makes it texturally more interesting to eat.

2 Toss all of the blueberries in the blueberry syrup, then set aside while you prepare the danishes.

3 Transfer the fromage blanc mousse into a bowl and loosen it with a hand whisk. Evenly distribute the fromage blanc mousse between the six danish shells, carefully spreading the mousse to fill the corners of the danish. You want the mousse to not quite reach the top of the danish.

4 Spoon a healthy amount of blueberries on top of the mousse in each danish, ensuring you get a nice mixture of cut and whole blueberries in each. I like the blueberries to be plentiful, such that they sit a little higher than the top of the danish. Serve immediately.

5 Finally, brush the exposed edges of the pastry with warmed nappage.

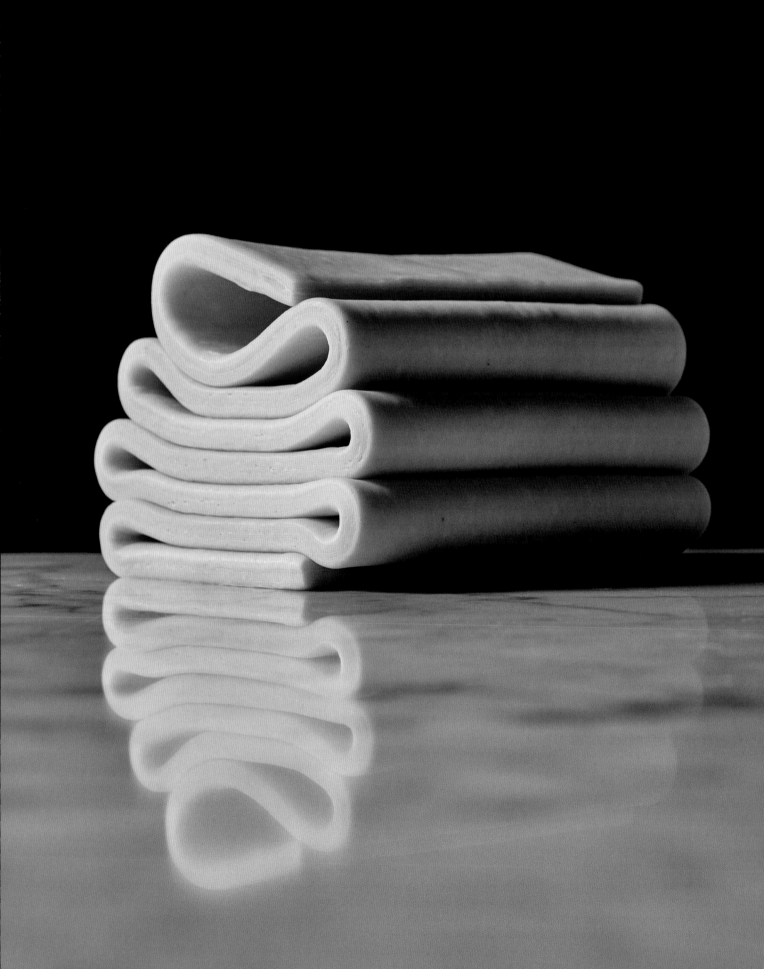

Lunch

Du Pain et des Idées

And so it was that I returned to Paris at the beginning of 2011 to embark, initially, on a one-month stage at Du Pain et des Idées.

Living in Paris felt like a dream. Early each morning, just as the sun was beginning to rise, I would walk the quiet Parisian streets to the boulangerie, the whole city lustrous in the golden hour. The only signs of life were the other boulangeries, already assiduously baking from pre-dawn hours in preparation for supply of baguettes and croissants to an awakening city.

I was stationed in the raw pastry kitchen. Luxuriously, the entire first floor of the boulangerie was dedicated to the cold production of dough and pastry for the viennoiseries. This meant no ovens, simply an enormous chilled marble benchtop, a laminoir, a large mixer and a wall of freezers and blast chillers. I worked under the Head Pastry Chef, Sebastien, and alongside Hyun-Jee, a very talented pastry chef from Korea, who exercised extreme patience with my poor French, and taught me many of the prep jobs required in the raw pastry kitchen (and also probably taught me most of my bakery-specific French language. As a result, I suspect I returned to Melbourne speaking French with a Korean accent...).

The days were tiring, but never have I felt quite so utterly fulfilled as I did for those weeks working at the boulangerie. Not only was I learning challenging new skills and techniques, I was doing it all in French. The work was physically demanding too; regularly we had to transport 20 kg (44 lb) bags of flour from the basement, up two narrow spiral staircases to the raw pastry kitchen. I was physically and mentally stimulated, I felt like I had finally found my thing.

After one month of staging at DPDI, I returned to Melbourne. To this day, I can't remember why exactly it was that I made the decision to leave Paris. But back in Melbourne, high on butter and pastry knowledge and French culture, I started to feel a bit restless ... I wanted to recreate the life I'd had a taste of in Paris, starting simply with a great croissant.

On my days off, I would visit bakeries, in search of something that reminded me of the sublime experience of eating a proper butter croissant, fresh from the oven. The search took me all over Melbourne, and each time, left me disillusioned. While Melbourne had rightly earned its reputation for serving some of the best coffee in the world, sadly it seemed that could not be said for its viennoiserie.

A seed of an idea started to form ...

Spring Pea and Goat's Curd Danish

YIELDS 6

6 blind-baked danish (page 93)

120 g seasoned goat's curd

pea tendrils and onion flowers, to garnish

orange and onion marmalade

salsa verde

pea and broad (fava) bean mix

Every spring, without fail, this danish gets a guernsey on the Lune counter. Classically, spring is a bit light-on when it comes to delicious in-season fruits. Luckily this is not the case for vegetables, and mother nature gifts us with some of the best edible greenery of the year. So, we celebrate it.

As per the danish recipes in the Morning Tea chapter, this one is blind baked, so follow the proving and baking instructions on page 93.

ORANGE AND ONION MARMALADE

2 oranges

30 g (2 tbsp) grapeseed oil

2 brown onions, sliced

160 g (5½ oz) raw sugar

120 g (4¼ oz) white wine vinegar

1 cinnamon stick

2 g coriander seeds

2 g allspice

2 g black peppercorns

salt, to taste

1 Peel the oranges then cut between the membranes to release the segments, doing this over a bowl to catch any juice that escapes (you'll want to use that, to really drive home the orange flavour in the marmalade).

2 Heat the grapeseed oil in a saucepan over a low heat, add the onions and sweat until translucent and starting to colour slightly. Add the raw sugar, stir through the onions and cook for a minute or so – you will notice it starts to become sticky.

3 Add the orange segments and cook for a minute, stirring, then add the reserved orange juice and white wine vinegar.

4 Tie the spices up in some muslin cloth (cheesecloth), then add them into the pan and cover with a cartouche.

5 Cook for 2 hours over the lowest heat, stirring every 15–20 minutes to stop the marmalade catching and burning on the bottom of the pan.

6 Once you have achieved a sticky marmalade consistency, add salt to taste, then transfer into a clean sealed container or sterilised jar and store in the fridge until required.

SALSA VERDE

1 bunch of mint

1 bunch of basil

1 bunch of chives, cut into 3

2 confit garlic cloves

75 g (2½ oz) capers, rinsed

lemon juice, to taste

about 100 g (3½ oz) olive oil

1 Pick and wash all the herbs. Place the garlic and capers in the bottom of a blender or food processor, followed by the picked herbs. Pour in a little lemon juice and about half of the oil (just enough liquid to allow everything to blend uniformly). Once the mixture has an even consistency, slowly pour in the remaining oil with the blender on high speed. This process needs to be **fast**. The longer the herbs are processed for, the higher chance that they will bruise and turn brown, so your salsa verde won't be so 'verde'.

2 Season to taste, and store in a sealed container in the fridge until required. →

PEA AND BROAD (FAVA) BEAN MIX

80 g (3 oz) broad (fava) beans, podded, blanched and coarsely chopped

120 g (7 oz) fresh peas, blanched and coarsely chopped

40 g (2 oz) salsa verde

salt, to taste

1   Combine all the ingredients, checking the seasoning.

FINISHING

1   Take your six cooled, unfilled blind-baked danish shells. Spoon 20 g (¾ oz) of the orange and onion marmalade into the base of each danish, spreading it out so there is even coverage.

2   Transfer your seasoned goat's curd into a piping bag and, for each danish, pipe about 20g (¾ oz) of goat's curd evenly over the top of the marmalade.

3   Carefully spoon 30 g (1 oz) of the pea and broad bean mix on top of the goat's curd, then garnish each danish with pea tendrils and onion flowers that have been lightly dressed in olive oil and seasoned. Serve immediately.

The Reuben

YIELDS 6

1 batch of pastry, rolled out and cut for croissants

100 g (3½ oz) pastrami, thinly sliced

75 g (2½ oz) sauerkraut, combined with 50 g (1¾ oz) of Russian dressing

75 g (2½ oz) Gruyère, finely grated

1 egg, beaten ('egg wash')

pickled cornichons, halved lengthways, to garnish

The original Lune was located in Melbourne's South East, where grocery stores are heavily influenced by the long-established Jewish community. As such, there were several incredible Jewish delicatessens nearby, which sparked the idea for a croissant based on the classic Reuben sandwich. Don't skimp on your pastrami for this one – source the best you can find!

While the pastrami and sauerkraut are synonymous with a Reuben sandwich, almost undoubtedly the russian dressing is the unsung hero of this recipe.

RUSSIAN DRESSING

1 egg yolk

8 Dijon mustard

3 g (0.1 oz) fresh horseradish, grated

3 g (0.1 oz) Worcestershire sauce

3 g (0.1 oz) Tabasco

4 g (0.14 oz) onion powder

pinch of paprika

pinch of salt

140 g (5 oz) neutral oil (e.g. grapeseed, canola)

35 g (1¼ oz) HP sauce

1   Blend the first eight ingredients together in a blender or food processor on high speed for 1 minute, then, while still blending, slowly start to drizzle in the oil. When you have incorporated about half of the oil, add a teaspoon of hot water, then continue to slowly pour in the remaining oil. Stir the HP sauce in by hand at the end. Refrigerate until required.

SHAPING

1   Reuben croissants are shaped in the same manner as the Ham and Gruyère (page 49), with the filling placed on top of the stretched raw pastry then rolled up.

2   To assemble the filling: at the wide end of one of the croissants, place 20 g (¾ oz) of thinly sliced pastrami, fluffed up (not squished into a tight ball). On top of the pastrami, place 20 g (¾ oz) of the dressed sauerkraut mixture. Finally, atop the sauerkraut, place 15 g (½ oz) of finely grated gruyère.

PROVE AND BAKE AS PER HAM AND GRUYERE WITH THE BELOW VARIATION SEE PAGE 49

1   Serve with half a pickled cornichon on a toothpick speared into the top of the Reuben croissant.

Spiced Cauliflower Bearclaw

YIELDS 6

1 batch of pastry, rolled and cut for pain au chocolat

pickled cauliflower

60 g (3 oz) Parmesan, shaved

roasted cauliflower

1 egg, beaten ('egg wash')

Several years ago, our Head Chef approached me with the idea of a savoury vegetarian pastry featuring cauliflower. Look, I appreciate cauliflower as much as the next person, but the prospect of a cauliflower pastry left me feeling a little underwhelmed. I'm not one to quell inspiration, however, so I gave the green light to develop the pastry.

Well, it was quite the unexpected success when it finally hit the menu, and I happily ate my words.

Whenever we reach out to our customers on social media and ask which vintage Lune pastries they'd like to see make a return to the menu, there are always a few voices that shout loudly to 'bring back the cauliflower bearclaw'.

If there's one sentence I never expected I would hear, it's **'bring back the cauliflower bearclaw'**.

But here it is, in all its glory.

This recipe yields more roasted and pickled cauliflower than you will need for the bearclaw recipes. The roasted cauliflower will also form the base for a delicious salad (think pomegranate seeds, chopped parsley, hazelnuts), and the pickled cauliflower is a great addition to a Ploughman's lunch spread or cheese board.

SPICE MIX

110 g (3¾ oz) hazelnuts

80 g (2¾ oz) white sesame seeds

2 tablespoons coriander seeds

2 tablespoons cumin seeds

2 tablespoons black peppercorns

1 tablespoon pink sea salt

1   Preheat your oven to 160°C fan (320°F).

2   Roast the hazelnuts and sesame seeds on two separate trays for 10 minutes or until fragrant and starting to colour. Remove from the oven and allow to cool.

3   Once the hazelnuts are cool, blitz in a food processor until finely chopped, but not so fine that the texture approaches a hazelnut meal. You want a bit of crunch and texture.

4   Toast the coriander seeds, cumin seeds and black peppercorns in a dry frying pan over a medium heat for about 2 minutes until aromatic, being careful not to burn them. Once toasted, either crush the spices together in a pestle and mortar, or blitz in a spice grinder.

5   Combine the nuts, seeds, spices and salt.

ROASTED CAULIFLOWER

vegetable oil

500 g (1 lb 2 oz) cauliflower, broken into tiny florets

salt and pepper, to taste

50 g (1¾ oz) spice mix (above)

1   Preheat your oven to 220°C fan (425°F).

2   Heat some vegetable oil in a large pan over a medium-high heat. Add the cauliflower florets, making sure not to overcrowd the pan (you don't want it to steam), and allow them to develop some colour (some little black spots are fine). Season well with salt and pepper.

3   Transfer the par-cooked florets to a large baking tray, spreading them out in a thin layer (again taking care not to overcrowd the tray), then load them into to the oven to roast for a few minutes. You're looking for lovely roasty caramelised colouring on the cauliflower. Remove from the oven and sprinkle with the spice mix. Allow to cool completely to room temperature. →

PICKLED CAULIFLOWER

500 g (1 lb 2 oz) caster (superfine) sugar

250 g (9 oz) water

500 g (1 lb 2 oz) white wine vinegar

10 g (⅓ oz) fennel seeds

10 g (⅓ oz) mustard seeds

20 g (¾ oz) salt

500 g (1 lb 2 oz) cauliflower, broken into tiny florets

PREPARE AT LEAST ONE DAY IN ADVANCE

1   Heat everything except the cauliflower in a large saucepan, allowing the sugar to dissolve.

2   Place the cauliflower florets in sterilised jars and carefully pour the hot pickling liquid over the top, ensuring that the florets are fully submerged. Seal the jars and allow to cool completely to room temperature before refrigerating. Steep for at least one day before using.

SHAPING

1   Carefully pick up each rectangle of pastry cut 9 cm by 12 cm (3½ cm by 4¾ cm) and stretch it to increase the length to approximately one and a half times its original length. The long sides of the rectangle will 'bow in' slightly, the top and bottom edges remaining their original 9 cm (3½ cm).

2   On the bottom half of the stretched pastry, place 10 g of pickled cauliflower, leaving a border of approximately 2 cm (1 in) from the bottom edge. Cover the pickled cauliflower with 10 g of shaved parmesan, and finally, 20 g of roasted cauliflower.

3   Taking the top edge of a bearclaw, fold the pastry 'lid' over the cauliflower filling to meet the bottom edge. Using the length of your index finger, press to flatten and secure the join. Repeat with remaining pastries.

4   Now using a paring knife, where the top and bottom edges have joined, make 3 small cuts of approximately 1 cm (½ in) through both layers of pastry. Repeat for all pastries.

5   Place the shaped bearclaws on a baking tray lined with baking paper, ensuring that they are evenly spaced, with enough room between them to allow for them to grow during proving and baking.

6   Reserve in the fridge until you are ready to start proving.

PROVING

1   Place your tray of shaped cauliflower bearclaws in your turned-off oven with a dish of boiling water in the bottom. Allow to prove for about 5 hours. The claws will start to open up, which is a good indication that they are ready to be baked.

BAKING

1   Remove the tray of proven bearclaws and the dish of water from the oven. Preheat your oven to to 210°C fan (410°F).

2   Using a soft-bristled pastry brush, carefully apply the egg wash, ensuring you don't use so much that it pools at the base of the bearclaw. Dust the top of the egg-washed pastry with some spice mix.

3   Bake the bearclaws for 5 minutes at 210°C fan (410°F), then knock your oven back to 160°C fan (320°F) and bake for a further 16 minutes. If you know your oven well and it has a hot spot, rotate your tray 180 degrees for the last 8 minutes.

4   Allow to cool for 10 minutes before serving.

Escargots

6 springform tins (ring only),
11 cm (4½ in) in diameter, greased
and lined with baking paper and
placed on a lined baking tray

1 batch of pastry, rolled out and
cut for escargot

1 egg, beaten ('egg wash')

While more traditionally treated as a sweet viennoiserie, at Lune we really lean on the escargot as a foundation for showcasing our savoury flavour combinations.

This particular pastry is by far the easiest to master the shaping of, and is also more forgiving when it comes to not-quite-so-perfectly-laminated pastry. Besides, who doesn't want to test out their new-found croissant skills on a pepperoni pizza escargot recipe?!

The three recipes that follow are arguably the most popular escargots that have appeared on the Lune counter over the years, regularly making reappearances.

PROVING

1   Place your tray of shaped escargots in your turned-off oven with a dish of boiling water in the bottom and allow to prove for 5–6 hours. They are ready when they are touching the sides of the springform ring.

BAKING

1   Remove the proven escargots and dish of water from your oven, then heat it to 210°C fan (410°F).

2   If you have already attempted the Cheese and Vegemite Escargot on page 51, you will remember that the escargot is the one of the only pastries where you almost want to be a little bit 'rough' in the egg-washing process. Ensuring that your pastry brush is generously drenched in egg wash, press very firmly on the top of the proven pastry with the flat of the pastry brush. Think of it as 'gluing the layers of the escargot together' – this will help prevent the centre spiralling out. Season the egg-washed escargots generously with sea salt and cracked black pepper.

3   Bake the escargots for 5 minutes at 210°C fan (410°F) then knock your oven back to 160°C fan (320°F) and bake for a further 16–20 minutes, again looking for an even colour to indicate that they are finished baking. Once again, rotate the tray 180 degrees in the final few minutes if you know your oven has a hot spot.

4   When you are happy with the colour, remove from oven and, using oven mitts, carefully remove the springform ring and allow to cool. Rest for at least 10 minutes before serving.

Escargot Variations

Cacio E Pepe Escargot

YIELDS 6

6 springform tins (ring only)
11 cm (4½ in) in diameter, greased
and lined with baking paper

1 batch of pastry, rolled and
cut for escargot

béchamel

100 g (3½ oz) Parmesan,
finely grated

black pepper, to taste

1 egg, beaten ('egg wash')

pecorino Romano, to garnish

Several years ago I was travelling in the USA, and had dinner with a friend at Rose's Luxury in Washington DC. Before the first course was served, they brought out a complimentary cacio e pepe-inspired monkey bread. It was still warm, and the sheer joy of pulling apart cheesy, peppery bread with a friend was not lost on either of us.

I returned to Melbourne from that trip and developed the Cacio e Pepe Escargot as a tribute to travel, adventure, inspiration in surprising places, and breaking bread with friends.

BÉCHAMEL

150 g (5 oz) milk

1 bay leaf

2 whole peppercorns

1 garlic clove

15 g (½ oz) butter

15 g (½ oz) plain (all-purpose)
flour

15 g (½ oz) Parmesan, grated

35 g (1¼ oz) pecorino, grated

cracked black pepper

pinch of salt

1   Pour the milk into a small saucepan, add the bay, peppercorns and garlic and place over a medium heat, but do not let it come to the boil. Allow to cool, then refrigerate overnight, allowing the aromats to infuse the milk.

2   The next day, strain the infused milk back into a saucepan and bring to a simmer, then remove from the heat.

3   In another small saucepan, melt the butter over a medium heat.

4   Add the flour to the melted butter and stir continuously with a whisk until fully combined – this is called a roux. Cook the roux over a medium heat until it just starts to catch on the bottom of the pan and becomes blonde in colour, and starts to smell just a *little* toasty.

5   While continuing to whisk the roux, begin to pour in the warmed milk. Once all the milk is added, bring the béchamel to a gentle boil and allow to boil for 1 minute, stirring continuously. Take off the heat and add the grated Parmesan and pecorino, stirring until they are fully combined. Finally, add a generous amount of cracked pepper and salt. Allow to cool to room temperature. Transfer to a sealed container and refrigerate.

SHAPING

1   Using a small offset palette knife, spread about 15 g (½ oz) of béchamel down each strip of pastry, stopping about 3 cm (1¼ in) before the end of each strip. Now cover the béchamel with 15 g (½ oz) of finely grated Parmesan on each strip, ensuring that you get even coverage along the whole length. Finally, crack a generous amount of black pepper over the grated parmesan.

2   Starting from the end furthest from you, roll up each strip one at a time, not too tightly, taking care to try and keep the grated Parmesan contained. Place each rolled escargot in a greased, lined springform ring, ensuring that it is in the centre of the ring so that it proves and bakes evenly.

PROVING AND BAKING   SEE PAGE 117

GARNISH

1   Finely grate a little mountain of pecorino on top of each escargot and, the piece de resistance, a generous amount of cracked black pepper. Because it isn't called cacio e pepe for nothing!

Escargots

Escargot Variations

Spanakopita Escargot

YIELDS 6

6 springform tins (ring only)
11 cm (4½ in) in diameter,
greased and lined with baking
paper and placed on a lined
baking tray

400 g (14 oz) cheese and
spinach mix

1 batch of pastry, rolled and
cut for escargot

1 egg, beaten ('egg wash')

Traditionally, the pastry element of spanakopita is made by layering sheets of filo brushed with either olive oil or melted butter, so it doesn't require a great stretch of the imagination to acknowledge that the classic spinach, herb and cheese filling will almost undoubtedly pair perfectly with buttery croissant pastry.

This recipe makes more cheese and spinach mix than you will need for six escargots, but it freezes wonderfully, so it's worth making up a big batch and keeping some stored in the freezer, for the next time you fancy whipping up Lune Spanakopitas!

CHEESE AND SPINACH MIX

1 bunch of English spinach

a small amount of olive oil

1 shallot, finely diced

1 garlic clove, minced

1 bunch of flat-leaf parsley,
finely chopped

1 bunch of mint, leaves picked
and finely chopped

1 bunch of dill, finely chopped

200 g (7 oz) feta, crumbled

200 g (7 oz) ricotta

1 egg

grated zest of 1 lemon

pinch of nutmeg

salt and pepper, to taste

1   Cut the stems off the spinach and wash the leaves well in lots of water: spinach can hold onto a lot of dirt, so I recommend filling up the sink and fully submerging the spinach in the water and moving it around with your hands for a little while, allowing the dirt to settle at the bottom of the sink.

2   Meanwhile, bring a large pot of water to the boil and prepare an ice bath (a large bowl of water filled with ice). As soon as the water is boiling rapidly, add the spinach and blanch for no more than 20 seconds, then transfer immediately to the ice bath. Strain all the water off the spinach, squeezing out as much water as you can. You can even do this in a clean tea towel – you really want the spinach as dry as possible. Finely chop the spinach.

3   Sweat the shallot and garlic in olive oil, then place all the cheese and spinach mix ingredients in the bowl of a stand mixer fitted with a flat beater and mix on slow speed, to simply bring everything together. Taste your mixture to check for seasoning – you will be surprised how much salt it can take! Transfer about 400 g (14 oz) of the mixture into one piping bag and refrigerate until required. Freeze the rest of the mixture in a sealed container, or pre-loaded into piping bags, ensuring the piping bag is well sealed and the tip hasn't been cut open.

SHAPING

1   Cut a 5 mm (¼ in) hole at the tip of the piping bag. Pipe a thick seam of the cheese and spinach mix along the length of each strip of pastry (about 50 g/1¾ oz of mixture for each escargot), stopping about 3 cm (1¼ in) before the end of the strip of pastry.

2   Starting from the end furthest from you, roll up each strip one at a time, not too tightly. Place each rolled escargot in a greased, lined springform ring, ensuring that it is in the centre of each ring so it proves and bakes evenly.

3   Reserve in the fridge until you are ready to start proving.

PROVING AND BAKING SEE PAGE 117

Escargots

123

Pepperoni Pizza Escargot

YIELDS 6

6 springform tins (ring only)
11 cm (4½ in) in diameter, greased
and lined with baking paper and
placed on a lined baking tray

1 batch of pastry, rolled and
cut for escargot

pizza sauce

210 g (7¼ oz) scamorza, grated

90 g (3¼ oz) pepperoni, halved
lengthways, then cut into very
thin semi-circles (1–2 mm-thick)

1 egg, beaten ('egg wash')

I love pepperoni pizza. It takes me straight back to my first ever night in New York City. Somewhere in the LES around the 2am mark, jetlagged, several drinks deep, catching up on life with old friends, I experienced my first NYC pizza slice. Bigger than the size of my head, dripping with oil, covered in thin discs of salty pepperoni whose edges had curled up and taken on a light and crispy quality. In that moment, I'm not sure anything had ever been more delicious than that slice of pizza.

Whenever I take a bite of a Lune Pepperoni Pizza escargot, if I close my eyes, I am instantly transported back to that magical Manhattan night.

PIZZA SAUCE

a small amount of olive oil

1 garlic clove, minced

1 small shallot, finely chopped

¼ teaspoon dried oregano

250 g (9 oz) tomato paste

100 g (3½ oz) water

¼ teaspoon table salt

1   Heat the olive oil in a frying pan, add the garlic and shallot and cook until soft and translucent, then add the oregano and tomato paste. Cook the tomato paste for a minute of two, before adding the water and salt. Cook over a medium heat for a few minutes, mixing well to fully incorporate the water.

2   Allow to cool, then blitz in a food processor to achieve a smooth consistency.

3   Transfer to a container and refrigerate until ready to use.

SHAPING

1   Using a small offset palette knife, spread about 15 g (½ oz) of pizza sauce down each strip of pastry, stopping about 3 cm (1¼ in) before the end of each strip. For each escargot, cover the pizza sauce with 35 g (1¼ oz) of grated scamorza, then place 15 g (½ oz) of pepperoni slices on top of the scamorza.

2   Starting from the end furthest from you, roll up each strip one at a time, not too tightly, taking care to not lose scamorza or slices of pepperoni in the process. Place each rolled escargot in a greased, lined springform ring, ensuring that it is in the centre of the ring so that it proves and bakes evenly.

PROVE AND BAKE AS PER ESCARGOT WITH THE BELOW VARIATION SEE PAGE 117

1   As soon as you take the pastries out of the oven, remove the rings and carefully flip pastries over while still very warm (I would recommend using a wide offset palette knife, the aim is to not allow the escargot to unravel); the pepperoni pizza escargot is served flat side up. Allow to rest for 5 minutes before garnishing.

GARNISH

buffalo mozzarella

micro basil (or regular basil, thinly sliced)

olive oil, for drizzling

1   Tear the buffalo mozzarella into odd sized and shaped pieces and place randomly on top of each escargot. Gently pick a few micro basil leaves and randomly garnish each escargot with a few leaves. Finally, drizzle a small amount of olive oil over each escargot, literally just before serving.

2   Serve immediately, and watch the lucky recipients react when they take their first bite – it's a surprising experience to eat something made with croissant pastry, that tastes so familiarly of something entirely different.

Afternoon Tea

In June 2012 I signed the lease on a tiny shop in Elwood, a seaside suburb in Melbourne's south.

I had an idea to start a micro bakery specialising in croissants, which I would supply exclusively to Melbourne's best espresso bars and cafés. Melbournians would be able to enjoy a good coffee and a good croissant together, at last.

I named the bakery Lune. The logo was a little rocket. Appropriate for so many reasons; my background in aerospace engineering, my love for the moon, the fact that the stereotypical* croissant is shaped like a crescent moon. Lune is a French word and modern-day croissants are attributed to the French. But little known is a story about a first anniversary gift from my boyfriend during my Formula One days. We travelled to Bruge for the occasion, and in the official Tin Tin store he bought me a framed print of the cover of *Objectif Lune*, a depiction of a cartoon rocket lifting off from the desert. Some time later, he mused that this would make a great name for a café, should I ever own one ...

The early days of Lune were, in a nutshell, incredibly challenging and utterly exhausting. Apart from the endless support offered by my incredible mum and dad, who would regularly come down to the shop and help with dishes, deliveries, simple prep work, and sometimes even just keep me company, the days were long and lonely. I would start at 5 am, bake, then deliver the pastries, returning to Lune around 9 am to begin preparation of the following day's pastries. A day of work would regularly conclude at about 9 pm, when I would subsequently fall into bed, in readiness for the next day. It was a 7-day business and I ended up in a cycle reminiscent of Groundhog Day, working 90 to 100 hours a week.

Simply put, it was wholly unsustainable. I also felt like I was missing an important piece of the puzzle with the business in its current format. For all the time, effort and love I was putting into making the croissants, I wasn't able to witness people enjoying them.

In October 2013 I closed the business for two weeks and returned to Paris, perhaps to seek inspiration and clarity on how Lune needed to change, both to fit my needs and ensure longevity.

My brother, Cam, travelling up the East Coast of Australia on a motorbike tour, had recently sold a café and was looking for his next project. I proposed to him that he join me at Lune and help me transform the business from a wholesale micro bakery to a little customer-facing retail shop. Two months later we opened the (barn) door to our first ever little line of customers ...

*In actual fact, in France, a crescent-shaped croissant indicates that it has not been made with real butter, instead with margarine or another vegetable-based fat.

Lamington Cruffin

YIELDS 6

6 cruffins, baked, unfilled

100 g (3½ oz) raspberry jam
(see note)

100 g (3½ oz) whipped cream

200 g (7 oz) desiccated
(shredded) coconut

Chocolate Ganache
(Essentials, see page 264)

The inspiration for this cruffin stems from my deep love of all things jam and cream. The love affair started at a young age when Dad introduced me to jam and runny cream on white bread (a treat we were *sometimes* allowed after lunch). The affair continued when jam and cream would be slathered all over crêpes, consumed in copious amounts every year on Shrove Tuesday. But let's be honest, it's all about scones with jam and cream (jam first, of course, because that is the only way to do it).

The Lamington is a longstanding and classic Australian baked treat. Replacing the sponge cake with croissant pastry, it is surprising how reminiscent of an actual lamington this cruffin is, proving that as long as the flavour profile hits the mark, we can use childhood memory as great inspiration for new pastry ideas at Lune.

WHIPPED CREAM

300 g (10½ oz) thickened cream

30 g (1 oz) caster
(superfine) sugar

¼ teaspoon vanilla extract
(optional)*

1   Whip the cream and sugar (and the vanilla extract, if using) in the bowl of a stand mixer fitted with the whisk attachment until it forms stiff peaks. Transfer into a piping bag.   →

CHEF NOTE   These days at Lune we make our own raspberry jam, but in the early days (the Elwood era), I used Bonne Maman raspberry jam. It is available all over the world, and for my money, it is hands-down the best commercially available raspberry jam. For this recipe, I would recommend using a well-made commercially available raspberry jam, but if you're a preserve wizard and have a delicious homemade one in your pantry, feel free to go off-piste!

*I've left the vanilla extract as an optional addition because I personally prefer the whipped cream without vanilla for this cruffin. But hey, we've all got our personal preference and I won't judge!

ASSEMBLING

1   Take 6 cruffins that have been resting out of the oven for a minimum of 15 minutes. As you are going to be piping fresh whipped cream into them, you do not want the cruffins to have any residual heat inside.

2   Using a paring knife, create a hole in the top of each cruffin by inserting the knife into the top of the cruffin, right in the centre of the cruffin spiral, making sure not to cut all the way through to the bottom. This incision will allow you to poke piping bags into the cruffin to fill it.

3   Put the raspberry jam in a piping bag. Place a single cruffin on a set of digital kitchen scales and 'tare' the scales to zero, then pipe 15 g (½ oz) of raspberry jam into the cruffin – you want the jam to be quite deep inside the cruffin, so make sure the opening of the piping bag is inserted quite far into the cruffin. Repeat this step for the rest of the cruffins.

4   Once all 6 cruffins have their raspberry jam, take a single cruffin and again place it on a set of digital scales and 'tare' the scales to zero. Pipe 15 g (½ oz) of whipped cream into the cruffin. Again, make sure the tip of the piping bag has been adequately inserted far enough into the cruffin, otherwise the cream will just start to disgorge out the top (and basically, we want as much cream inside as possible, for pure eating pleasure!). Repeat this step for the rest of the cruffins.

5   Transfer the desiccated coconut into a small bowl.

6   Check to make sure that your ganache is still a nice thin liquid consistency and hasn't started to cool and thicken (if it has, you can put the heatproof bowl over a small saucepan filled with a few centimetres of simmering water and whisk the ganache until it melts to the desired consistency).

7   Holding the bottom half of a cruffin, dip the top in the ganache, turning it around to get good coverage, then remove from the ganache and turn it around a few times in a 360-degree motion to allow any excess ganache to drip off.

8   Immediately dip the ganache-covered cruffin top into the desiccated coconut. Transfer to a wire baking rack and repeat for the remaining cruffins.

Lamington cruffins do not have to be served immediately. In fact, they benefit from a short period of rest time to allow the ganache to firm up a little. They can be served up to an hour after assembly.

PBJ Cruffin

YIELDS 6

6 cruffins, baked, unfilled

Cinnamon Sugar (Essentials, see page 265)

Peanut Butter Crème Pâtissière (Essentials, see page 263)

120 g (4¼ oz) raspberry jam

Don't tell the others (because you're not meant to have a favourite kid), but the PBJ Cruffin is hands-down my favourite. It's the perfect balance of fun, nostalgic, and most importantly, it's super delicious.

As per the Lamington Cruffin recipe, feel free to use homemade raspberry jam, but for my money, the Bonne Maman raspberry jam has the perfect balance of sweet and tart, and its consistency works wonderfully for the PBJ cruffin.

PREPARING THE FILLING

1 Just before assembling the cruffins, take the crème pâtissière from the fridge, remove the cling film, and loosen the custard with a whisk. Transfer about 130 g (4½ oz) of the crème pâtissière into a piping bag (this will be enough to fill 6 PBJ cruffins, if you plan to make more than this, allow for 20 g/¾ oz per cruffin). Transfer the remaining into a sealed container and reserve in the fridge.

2 Transfer the jam into a piping bag.

ASSEMBLING

1 Take 6 cruffins that have been resting out of the oven for about 10 minutes. While they are still warm, gently toss each cruffin in cinnamon sugar, turning it to make sure you achieve full coverage, then shake off any excess sugar. After each one has been tossed in the sugar, return it to the wire cooling rack. Cool for 20 minutes before proceeding.

2 Using a paring knife, create a hole in the top of each cruffin by inserting the knife into the top of the cruffin, right in the centre of the cruffin spiral, making sure not to cut all the way through to the bottom. This incision will allow you to poke piping bags into the cruffin to fill it.

3 Place a single cruffin on a set of digital kitchen scales and 'tare' the scales to zero, then pipe 20 g (¾ oz) of crème pâtissière into the cruffin – as you are going to be piping jam in as well, ensure the tip of the piping bag is inserted quite far into the cruffin before piping. Repeat this step for the rest of the cruffins.

4 Now take a cruffin and again place it on a set of digital scales and 'tare' the scales to zero. Pipe 20 g (¾ oz) of raspberry jam into the cruffin. Again, make sure the tip of the piping bag has been inserted far enough into the cruffin before you begin piping. Repeat this step for the rest of the cruffins.

5 Finally, for presentation purposes, pipe a small button of jam right in the centre on the top of each cruffin.

While it's possible to serve the PBJ Cruffin up to several hours after they have been assembled, for an unforgettable experience that will bring you childlike happiness, eat immediately, while the pastry is still slightly warm. It will be the best hot jam donut you've ever had.

Pumpkin Pie Cruffin

YIELDS 6

6 cruffins, baked, unfilled

100 g (3½ oz) maple syrup gel

200 g (7 oz) pumpkin pie filling

Cinnamon Sugar
(Essentials, see page 265)

cinnamon cream

cinnamon, to dust

This one always gets wheeled out in October or November at Lune; sometimes our nod to Halloween, and sometimes Thanksgiving (two holidays that are traditionally not celebrated in Australia, but are fast gaining popularity).

If you are in the mood to make an actual pumpkin pie too, this recipe makes enough quantity of the pumpkin pie filling for you to fill six cruffins and a blind-baked tart shell! Keep in mind that because the pumpkin pie filling is technically already cooked, all you need to do is transfer the pumpkin pie filling into a blind-baked tart shell and serve!

THE PUMPKIN PUREE

1 butternut squash (pumpkin), halved lengthways and seeds scooped out

PREPARE A DAY IN ADVANCE

1   Preheat your oven to 220°C fan (425°F) and line a baking tray with baking paper.

2   Place the squash halves, cut side down, on the lined baking tray. Cover the whole tray with foil. Roast for 1 hour, until the flesh of the squash is very soft and tender, but not burnt.

3   Remove from the oven and allow to cool. When the squash is cool enough to touch, scoop out the flesh and discard the skin. Transfer the pumpkin flesh to a blender or food processor and blend until very smooth. If there are still some chunky or stringy bits you may need to pass it through a sieve to get it super smooth.

4   The recipe for pumpkin pie filling calls for 350 g (12 oz) of pumpkin puree, so weigh this into a bowl (or a sealed container, stored in the fridge, if you plan to make the pumpkin pie filling later), and transfer the remaining mix into a sealed container and freeze, convenient for when you have a pumpkin pie cruffin craving at a later date!

PUMPKIN PIE FILLING

180 g (6⅓ oz) milk

1 teaspoon ground cinnamon

½ teaspoon ground ginger

¼ teaspoon ground nutmeg

¼ teaspoon ground cloves

pinch of ground cardamom

110 g (3¾ oz) brown sugar

110 g (3¾ oz) egg yolk
(about 6 egg yolks)

300 g (10½ oz) thickened cream

3 gelatine leaves
(gold strength), soaked

350 g (12 oz) pumpkin puree

50 g (1¾ oz) maple syrup

pinch of salt

PREPARE A DAY IN ADVANCE

1   Preheat your oven to 200°C fan (400°F).

2   Put the milk and spices in a small saucepan, place over a medium heat, and heat until it's just about to reach boiling point.

3   Meanwhile, whisk the brown sugar with the egg yolks in a bowl to combine. Pour the hot milk over the yolks, whisking constantly to incorporate. Add the cold cream and blend the whole mixture with a stick blender.

4   Strain the mixture into a high-sided brownie tray, cover with foil, and bake for about 20 minutes, until the mixture looks split and scrambled, and liquid is starting to separate (it's not going to look right, but trust me, it is!).

5   Remove from the oven, transfer to a blender and add the gelatine, then blend until the mixture has re-emulsified and looks smooth and homogenous again. Add the pumpkin puree, maple syrup and salt to the blender and pulse until the mixture comes together. Transfer into a container and allow to set in the fridge overnight.

6   Once set, transfer 200 g (7 oz) of the pumpkin pie filling into a piping bag. Freeze the remaining filling for when you next feel like making Pumpkin Pie Cruffins, or just a good old simple pumpkin pie! →

MAPLE SYRUP GEL

1 teaspoon agar powder

250 g (9 oz) cold water

100 g (3½ oz) maple syrup

1 Mix the agar powder with the cold water in a small saucepan and cook over a medium heat, stirring until the agar is fully dissolved. Bring to the boil and boil for 5 minutes.

2 'Tare' a small heatproof measuring jug on your kitchen scales and weigh 50 g (1¾ oz) of the boiled water with agar into the jug. Discard the rest of the boiled water (this is an important step – you only actually need 50 g/1¾ oz of the water, I have just scaled these two ingredients up because it is important to be accurate with the agar powder, and weighing one or two grams with normal kitchen scales is not possible). Transfer this 50 g (1¾ oz) of agar water back into the small saucepan and add 50 g (1¾ oz) of the maple syrup. Bring to the boil, then remove from the heat, pour into a heatproof bowl and allow to cool to room temperature. Once cooled, transfer to a blender, add the remaining 50 g (1¾ oz) of maple syrup and blitz until smooth. Transfer to a piping bag.

CINNAMON CREAM

300 g (10½ oz) double (heavy) cream

½ teaspoon ground cinnamon, plus a little extra for dusting

1 Transfer the cream and cinnamon into the bowl of a stand mixer fitted with the whisk attachment, and whisk to form soft peaks. You want the cream to hold – watch that it doesn't become thin and runny. If it does, you will need to whisk it by hand to bring it back to a thick consistency.

ASSEMBLING

1 Take 6 cruffins that have been resting out of the oven for about 10 minutes. While they are still warm, gently toss each cruffin in cinnamon sugar, turning it to make sure you achieve full coverage, then shake off any excess sugar. After each one has been tossed in the sugar, return it to the wire cooling rack. Cool for 20 minutes before proceeding.

2 Using a paring knife, create a hole in the top of each cruffin by inserting the knife into the top of the cruffin, right in the centre of the cruffin spiral, making sure not to cut all the way through to the bottom. This incision will allow you to poke piping bags into the cruffin to fill it.

3 Place a single cruffin on a set of digital kitchen scales and 'tare' the scales to zero, then pipe 15 g (½ oz) of the maple syrup gel into the cruffin – as you are going to be piping the pumpkin pie filling in as well, ensure the tip of the piping bag is inserted quite far into the cruffin before piping. Repeat this step for the rest of the cruffins.

4 Once all six cruffins have their maple syrup gel, take a single cruffin and again place it on a set of digital scales and 'tare' the scales to zero. Pipe 30 g (1 oz) of pumpkin pie filling into the cruffin. Again, you're going to need to make sure the tip of the piping bag has been inserted far enough into the cruffin before you begin piping. Repeat this step for the rest of the cruffins.

5 The pumpkin pie cruffin is topped with a beautiful rustic quenelle of cinnamon cream. Using a dessertspoon, scoop a healthy amount of the cream and dollop it on top of each cruffin. It doesn't need to be perfect; in fact, in this instance, I really enjoy the individuality of the cruffins with a non-uniform cream garnish.

6 Finally, take a tiny pinch of cinnamon between your thumb and forefinger and sprinkle delicately over the top of the cream, being very careful not to overdo it!

Serve immediately to your happy little trick or treaters (or your guests, who will no doubt be giving thanks for the efforts you have gone to here!).

Passionfruit Coconut Cruffin

YIELDS 6

6 cruffins, baked, unfilled

passionfruit sugar

passionfruit whip

100 g (3½ oz) passionfruit jam

flaked coconut, to garnish

meringue shards, to garnish

This cruffin oozes serious summer vibes. With a good whack of Malibu in both the passionfruit whip and the jam, its maybe one to save for the over 18s …

The recipe for the passionfruit jam gives you more than you need for six cruffins, but let's be honest, no one is going to be upset with a bit of leftover passionfruit jam to spread on their butter-drenched toast, sandwich between a Victoria sponge, or even as a fancy filling to zhuzh up a batch of good old-fashioned butterfly cakes (one of my favourite treats!).

PASSIONFRUIT JAM

175 g (6 oz) caster (superfine) sugar

7 g (¼ oz) pectin

250 g (9 oz) passionfruit pulp

50 g (1¾ oz) Malibu

PREPARE A DAY IN ADVANCE

1 Mix the sugar and pectin in a small bowl and set aside.

2 Put the passionfruit pulp and Malibu in a small saucepan and bring to the boil. Once this mixture is boiling, add the sugar and pectin mix and whisk to dissolve. Boil the jam until it reaches an appropriate consistency. You can test it the old-school way by putting a saucer in the freezer when you begin making the jam, then when you want to test the setting point of the jam, spoon a dollop of jam onto the saucer, pop it back into the freezer and take your jam off the heat momentarily. If the jam is ready, it should have formed a bit of a skin, which, when gently pushed with your finger, is a bit wrinkly. If it's still runny and no skin has formed, pop it back on the heat and test again in another 5 minutes with the cold saucer.

3 Transfer 100 g (3½ oz) of the jam into a heatproof bowl and the rest into a sterilised jar. Once the jam in the bowl has cooled completely, transfer it to a piping bag.

PASSIONFRUIT WHIP

100 g (3½ oz) passionfruit pulp

20 g (¾ oz) Malibu

40 g (1½ oz) caster (superfine) sugar

10 g (⅓ oz) milk

40 g (1½ oz) thickened cream

80 g (2¾ oz) coconut cream

double (heavy) cream, as required

1 teaspoon xantham gum

PREPARE A DAY IN ADVANCE

1 Put the passionfruit pulp, Malibu and sugar in a small saucepan and bring to the boil. Allow to reduce by a third, then reduce the heat to low. Add the milk, thickened cream and coconut cream and bring to the boil again, reducing ever so slightly.

2 Pour the reduction into a heatproof bowl, allow to cool to room temperature then cover with cling film and refrigerate overnight.

3 On the day you plan to serve the cruffins, weigh how much mixture you have then transfer this chilled mixture to the bowl of a stand mixer fitted with a whisk attachment. Add half the weight of the mixture in double (heavy) cream (i.e., if your mixture weighs 200 g/7 oz, add 100 g/3½ oz of double cream to the bowl of the stand mixer), then whip until it reaches a light consistency. Transfer to a piping bag. →

MERINGUE SHARDS

90 g (3¼ oz) egg white
(the whites of 3 large eggs)

90 g (3¼ oz) caster
(superfine) sugar

90 g (3¼ oz) pure icing
(powdered) sugar, sifted

10 g (⅓ oz) cornflour
(cornstarch), sifted

PREPARE A DAY IN ADVANCE

1   Preheat your oven to 80°C fan (180°F).

2   Whip the egg whites to soft peaks in the bowl of a stand mixer fitted with the whisk attachment. Once they have reached soft peak stage, gradually add the caster (superfine) sugar while the whites are still whipping, one tablespoon at a time. Once all the caster sugar has been added, do the same with the icing (powdered) sugar and cornflour (cornstarch).

3   Spread the meringue mixture on a baking tray lined with baking paper. Using an offset palette knife, try to get the meringue spread as thinly as possible. Bake for 1 hour 15 minutes. Allow to cool completely to room temperature before breaking into random-shaped shards of about 2 cm (¾ in) (similar in shape to a coconut flake).

PASSIONFRUIT SUGAR

250 g (9 oz) caster
(superfine) sugar

10 g (⅓ oz) freeze-dried
passionfruit powder

1   Combine the sugar and passionfruit powder in a bowl, mixing thoroughly with a whisk to ensure that the powder is evenly distributed. (Leftover passionfruit sugar can be stored in a sealed container for use at a later date. Sift the sugar before storing, to remove any flakes of croissant pastry that may have found their way into the sugar.)

ASSEMBLING

1   Take 6 cruffins that have been resting out of the oven for about 5 minutes. While they are still warm, gently toss each cruffin in the passionfruit sugar, turning it to make sure you achieve full coverage, then shake off any excess sugar. After each one has been tossed in the sugar, return it to the wire cooling rack. Cool for 20 minutes before proceeding.

2   Using a paring knife, create a hole in the top of each cruffin by inserting the knife into the top of the cruffin, right in the centre of the cruffin spiral, making sure not to cut all the way through to the bottom. This incision will allow you to poke piping bags into the cruffin to fill it.

3   Place a single cruffin on a set of digital kitchen scales and 'tare' the scales to zero, then pipe 25 g (1 oz) of passionfruit whip into the cruffin, ensuring the tip of the piping bag is inserted quite far into the cruffin before applying pressure to the piping bag. Repeat this step for the rest of the cruffins.

4   Now take a cruffin and again place it on a set of digital scales and 'tare' the scales to zero. Pipe 20 g (¾ oz) of passionfruit jam into the cruffin, following the passionfruit whip. Again, make sure the tip of the piping bag has been inserted far enough into the cruffin before you begin piping. Repeat for the rest of the cruffins.

5   Once all cruffins have been piped with both the passionfruit whip and jam, finish off each one by piping a little button of the whip on top of the cruffins.

6   Finally, alternating between flaked coconut and meringue shards, garnish the top of each cruffin with a mixture of both (7 to 8 pieces in total), gently pressed into the button of passionfruit whip, standing up vertically.

Perfect beverage pairing; a piña colada!

Banoffee Pie Cruffin

YIELDS 6

6 cruffins, baked, unfilled

'marie biscuit' sugar

Dulce de Leche, prepared a day in advance (Essentials, see page 264)

banana crème diplomat

dark cocoa powder

150 g (5¼ oz) double cream, whipped

dark chocolate, grated

The original Lune banoffee pie offering was actually a request from my good friend Zoe Foster-Blake. Zoe and her husband, Hamish, had ordered banoffee pie on their first date at Fratelli Fresh in Sydney. Zoe asked if I could create a Lune pastry reminiscent of that fateful dessert. In its first incarnation, the banoffee pie was a blind-baked danish, filled with dulce de leche, then topped with slices of fresh banana and, finally, lashings of whipped cream.

The banoffee pie cruffin is a slightly more refined version of the original danish. If you don't feel like being refined, please feel free to blind-bake six danishes, replace the banana cream in this recipe with slices of fresh banana, and fill the danish as per the mouth-watering description above!

BANANA CRÈME DIPLOMAT

170 g (6 oz) thickened cream

100 g (3½ oz) icing (powdered) sugar, sifted

150 g (5 oz) banana puree

40 g (1½ oz) milk

2 egg yolks

70 g (2½ oz) caster (superfine) sugar

pinch of sea salt

15 g (½ oz) cornflour (cornstarch), sifted

1 gelatine leaf (gold strength), soaked

30 g (1 oz) butter

PREPARE A DAY IN ADVANCE

1   In the bowl of a stand mixer fitted with the whisk attachment, whip 120 g (4¼ oz) of the thickened cream and icing (powdered) sugar to soft peaks. Set aside for later.

2   In a blender, combine the banana puree, the remaining thickened cream and the milk to a smoothie-like consistency.

3   In a mixing bowl, whisk together the egg yolks, caster (superfine) sugar, salt and cornflour (cornstarch), whisking well to combine, until the mixture is pale and light.

4   Add the banana puree mixture to the egg yolk mixture, whisk to combine, then transfer to a medium saucepan.

5   Set over a medium heat and cook the mixture, stirring constantly with a heatproof spatula or wooden spoon, for 3 minutes until the mixture is very thick and gluey.

6   Once the mixture has reached this consistency, add the soaked gelatine leaf and the butter, stirring to melt the butter and incorporate it into the mixture.

7   Transfer this mix to a heatproof bowl and allow to cool to room temperature. Once it has cooled completely, fold through the whipped cream. Cover and put in fridge overnight.

8   Just before assembling the cruffins, take the banana crème diplomat out of the fridge and loosen it with a whisk, then load into a piping bag.

9   Transfer the dulce de leche to a piping bag. →

'MARIE BISCUIT' SUGAR

100 g (3½ oz) caster (superfine) sugar

250 g (9 oz) marie biscuits

1   Blitz the marie biscuits and sugar in a food processor to a very fine crumb. Transfer to a container. The sugar will keep as long as the 'use by' date on the marie biscuits!

2   Leftover marie biscuit sugar can be stored in a sealed container for use at a later date. Sift the sugar before storing, to remove any flakes of croissant pastry that may have found their way into the sugar.

ASSEMBLING

1   Take 6 cruffins that have been resting out of the oven for about 5 minutes. While they are still warm, gently toss each cruffin in the 'marie biscuit' sugar, turning it to make sure you achieve full coverage, then shake off any excess sugar. After each one has been tossed in the sugar, return it to the wire cooling rack. Cool for 20 minutes before proceeding.

2   Using a paring knife, create a hole in the top of each cruffin by inserting the knife into the top of the cruffin, right in the centre of the cruffin spiral, making sure not to cut all the way through to the bottom. This incision will allow you to poke piping bags into the cruffin to fill it.

3   Place a single cruffin on a set of digital kitchen scales and 'tare' the scales to zero, then pipe 30 g (1 oz) of banana crème diplomat into the cruffin, ensuring the tip of the piping bag is inserted quite far into the cruffin before piping. Repeat this step for the rest of the cruffins.

4   Now take a cruffin and again place it on a set of digital scales and 'tare' the scales to zero. Pipe 10 g (⅓ oz) of dulce de leche into the cruffin. Again, make sure the tip of the piping bag has been inserted far enough into the cruffin before you begin piping. Repeat for the rest of the cruffins.

5   Sift a light dusting of dark cocoa powder over the top of the cruffins.

6   Pipe 7 small double-cream kisses in a flower formation on top of each cruffin, then finely grate a small amount dark chocolate over the top of the double cream kisses.

Whether you've gone to the effort to make the banana crème diplomat, or you've simply opted for the original Lune banoffee pie danish, if this was their first-date dessert, it's no surprise that Zoë and Hamish are now happily married with two beautiful children! Thanks for the inspiration, Zoë (in life, and pastry!).

CHEF NOTE If you don't live in Australia or the UK, you may not have heard of marie biscuits. Fear not, there's nothing fancy or gourmet about the good old marie biscuit! It's considered a pretty basic pantry staple, a very simple baked vanilla biscuit, found in the biscuit aisle of the supermarket!

Snickers Cruffin

6 cruffins, baked, unfilled

Peanut Butter Crème Pâtissière
(Essentials, see page 263)

Salted Caramel
(Essentials, see page 264)

Milk Chocolate Ganache (adapted
from Essentials, see page 264)

The Snickers Cruffin wasn't originally on my recipe list for the book, but I've since realised that literally all the necessary components already appear in the Essential Recipes chapter, so I thought I'd sling you a bonus!

It was also one of the first cruffins to hit the counter at Lune, all the way back in 2014, so it would be a bit remiss to not include it.

PREPARING THE PEANUT BUTTER CRÈME PÂTISSIÈRE

1   Just before assembling the cruffins, take the crème pâtissière from the fridge, remove the cling film, and loosen the custard with a whisk. Transfer about 130 g (4½ oz) of the crème pâtissière into a piping bag (this will be enough to fill 6 PBJ cruffins – if you plan to make more than this, allow for 20 g/¾ oz per cruffin). Transfer the remaining crème pâtissière into a sealed container and reserve in the fridge.

PREPARE THE GANACHE WITH THE BELOW VARIATION   SEE PAGE 264

1   Substitute milk chocolate for the dark chocolate in the Essentials recipe. Once the ganache has cooled completely to room temperature, transfer into a piping bag, ready for assembly. Keep at room temperature – if you refrigerate the ganache it will lose its beautiful shine, and be very stiff and therefore difficult to pipe. It is important that you've allowed the ganache to firm up a little though, or it will not hold its shape when piped.

ASSEMBLING

Garnish

icing (powdered) sugar,
for dusting

finely chopped peanuts

1   Take 6 cruffins that have been resting out of the oven for a minimum of 15 minutes. Using a paring knife, create a hole in the top of each cruffin by inserting the knife into the top of the cruffin, right in the centre of the cruffin spiral, making sure not to cut all the way through to the bottom. This incision will allow you to poke piping bags into the cruffin to fill it.

2   Place a single cruffin on a set of digital kitchen scales and 'tare' the scales to zero, then pipe 15 g (½ oz) of salted caramel into the cruffin, ensuring that the tip of the piping bag is inserted quite far into the cruffin before piping. Repeat this step for the rest of the cruffins.

3   Now take a cruffin and again place it on a set of digital scales and 'tare' the scales to zero. Pipe 25 g (1 oz) of peanut butter crème pâtissière into the cruffin. Again, make sure the tip of the piping bag has been inserted far enough into the cruffin before you begin piping. Repeat this step for the rest of the cruffins.

4   Once the cruffins have all been filled with both salted caramel and peanut butter crème pâtissière, dust them all lightly with icing sugar.

5   Cut a hole of about 5 mm (¼ in) in the tip of the chocolate ganache piping bag, then starting with the tip of the piping bag just inside the top of the cruffin, pipe a button of ganache about 2 cm (¾ in) in diameter. Make sure the button also sits a little proud of the top of the cruffin.

6   Finally, transfer your finely chopped peanuts into a small bowl and, one by one, gently dip the ganache into the chopped peanuts, ensuring good coverage while not flattening the ganache.

Okay, you can devour them now!

Four-Cheese Torsade

YIELDS 8

1 batch of pastry, rolled out
and cut for torsades

1 egg, beaten ('egg wash')

250 g (9 oz) blue cheese
béchamel

160 g (5½ oz) Gruyère,
finely grated

160 g (5½ oz) pecorino,
finely grated

80 g (2¾ oz) Raclette,
finely grated

piment d'Espelette, to garnish

black pepper, to taste

So you're the type of person that digs a savoury snack in the afternoon instead? Don't worry, I've got you covered. Torsade is a fancy French term for 'twist' and this delicious twist totally lives up to its fancy name.

It celebrates four different cheeses (we don't like to do things by halves at Lune), and makes for an excellent solo afternoon snack, or equally will play the starring role on your dinner-party cheese platter.

BLUE CHEESE BÉCHAMEL

200 g (7 oz) milk

1 bay leaf

2 black peppercorns

1 garlic clove

20 g (¾ oz) butter

20 g (¾ oz) plain (all-purpose)
flour

55 g (2 oz) blue cheese, grated

5 g (0.2 oz) pecorino, grated

pinch of salt

1   Pour the milk into a small saucepan, add the bay, peppercorns, and garlic and place over a medium heat, but do not let it come to the boil. Allow to cool, then refrigerate for several hours, to infuse the milk.

2   Strain the infused milk back into a saucepan and bring to a simmer, then remove from the heat. In another small saucepan, melt the butter over a medium heat. Add the flour to the melted butter and stir continuously with a whisk until fully combined, to create a roux. Cook the roux over a medium heat until it just starts to catch on the bottom of the pan and becomes blonde in colour, and starts to smell just a little toasty. Continuing to whisk the roux, begin to pour in the warmed milk. Once all the milk is added, bring the béchamel to a gentle boil and allow to boil for 1 minute, stirring continuously. Take off the heat and add the blue cheese and pecorino, stirring until they are fully combined. Finally, add a generous amount of cracked pepper and salt. Allow to cool to room temperature then transfer to a piping bag. If you are not going to use it immediately, refrigerate.

PROVING

1   As the torsade is technically only one layer of pastry, it proves a little faster than the other shapes.

2   Place your tray of shaped torsades in your turned-off oven with a dish of boiling water in the bottom, and allow to prove for 4–5 hours.   →

PREPARING PROVEN TORSADES FOR BAKING

1 Remove the tray of proven torsades and the dish of water from the oven. Preheat your oven to 210°C fan (410°F).

2 Brush the torsades gently with the egg wash, being careful not to damage the layers of pastry.

3 Cut a 5 mm (¼ in) hole in the tip of the piping bag filled with blue cheese béchamel and pipe a thick seam of béchamel down the centre of each torsade (about 30 g/1 oz). Sprinkle 20 g (¾ oz) of Gruyère on top of the béchamel for each torsade, evenly distributed along the full length, followed in the same manner by 20 g (¾ oz) of pecorino, then finally 10 g (⅓ oz) of grated Raclette. You want to make sure each mouthful of the pastry includes all of the cheeses (we've promised a four-cheese torsade after all!).

BAKING

1 Bake the torsades for 5 minutes at 210°C fan (410°F) then knock your oven back to 160°C fan (320°F) and bake for a further 16–20 minutes, looking for an even colour to indicate that they are finished baking. If you know your oven has a hot spot, rotate the tray 180 degrees for the final few minutes.

2 When the cheese is has taken on a beautiful golden hue, and is starting to form crispy edges, remove from the oven.

3 Take a generous pinch of piment d'Espelette and sprinkle over the top of each baked torsade.

4 Allow to rest for 5 minutes before serving (the combination of the smell of melted cheese and buttery pastry will be almost irresistible, but trust me, it's worth the painful 5-minute wait!).

Dinner

It only took a few weeks for the line to get pretty out of control. Word spreads fast, it would seem.

At first, there were a dozen or so customers waiting when we opened the doors at 8 am. People started arriving earlier, and *earlier*, but Cam and I would work with the blinds down until opening time, so we had little idea what was going on outside the front of the shop. One morning, around 6 am, we poked our heads out the door, and were shocked to see that a line had already formed!

Due to the size of the bakery (and the number of hours in a day!), the quantity of pastries we could produce in a single day capped out at approximately 500. But, with the demand growing, each day we would sell out within an hour of opening. So, we introduced a ticketing system.

At 6:30 am Cam would open a little service window and hand out numbered raffle tickets to each person in line. A raffle ticket entitled the holder to purchase a maximum of 6 pastries. With this system we knew how many customers would be guaranteed to secure their Lune haul. Most days, every ticket holder would buy the full quota of 6 pastries. Often 30 or 40 people (beyond those who were guaranteed) would still take a raffle ticket, knowing they had little chance of success, but they would hang around until we sold out, holding on to slim hope. Regularly, if someone missed out one day, they would arrive hours earlier the following day, determined not to miss out this time.

On a couple of noteworthy occasions the police arrived, suspicious of the early morning activity in an otherwise quiet residential street. In a Seinfeld-inspired moment, one particularly ill-mannered customer was firmly told 'No croissant for you'. But maybe the greatest legend of the Lune line occurred on the day of the Victorian State Election in 2014. A poor, unsuspecting gentleman arrived at the front of the Lune queue after waiting several hours, and confused, asked where the voting booths were.

Toward the end of the Elwood era, a set of customers would regularly arrive to begin queueing up before Cam and I even started work, as early as 2:30 am. It was a wild couple of years. The adrenalin that came from the excitement around Lune kept us going, but the days were long and physically exhausting, and again, Lune found itself in yet another unsustainable model. Not only was it going to be impossible for Cam and I to maintain the crazy hours of work, but we were starting to get a bad reputation. (Incorrect) rumours began to spread that we were purposely limiting the number of pastries to drive demand.

It was time to think a little bigger …

The Pulled Pork Croissant

YIELDS 5

1 batch of pastry, rolled out and cut for croissants

tomato chilli jam

100 g (3½ oz) pulled pork, shredded

50 g (1¾ oz) manchego, grated

50 g (1¾ oz) queso fresco, grated

5 picked guindilla peppers, to garnish

1 egg, beaten ('egg wash')

cracked black pepper

This is a great one for using leftover pulled pork (carnitas)!

In the early days of Lune, I lived above the bakery on a little mezzanine, with just enough room for a bed, a couch and a TV. From time to time, my good friend, Matt Perger, would come over for dinner and watch the F1 Grands Prix with me.

One Sunday night Matt showed up armed with his famous pulled pork. He supplied dinner on the proviso that I would make him a pulled pork croissant with the leftovers. It was such a success that we named it the MP3 (Matt Perger Pulled Pork) and supplied it at the Melbourne International Coffee Expo to celebrate Matt's entry in the World Barista Championships.

Included below is Matt's original pulled pork recipe – I've left it word-for-word, so you too can experience the joy of a Matt Perger recipe!

You'll have far more chilli jam than you need for five pulled pork croissants, but you can store any leftover jam in sterilised jars and enjoy it with all that leftover pulled pork!

MATT PERGER'S PULLED PORK

2 onions, very finely diced

6 garlic cloves, crushed

2 tablespoons olive oil

2 kg (4 lb 8 oz) pork butt (shoulder)

1 tablespoon ground cumin

1 tablespoon chilli powder (preferably hot and smoked, like ancho)

juice and pared rind of 1 orange

juice of 2 limes

¼ cup red wine vinegar

3 bay leaves

a liberal amount of salt

black pepper

1 litre (2 ⅛ pints) chicken stock

1–2 tablespoons oregano (depends on how Italian you want to go)

PREPARE A DAY IN ADVANCE

1   Sweat the onions and garlic in the olive oil real slow in a saucepan for at least 45 minutes.

2   Preheat the oven to 100–120°C fan (210–250°F). Trim off the excess pork fat and cut into roughly 3 cm (1¼ in) chunks. Sear the pork in three batches in another pan (a cast-iron casserole dish is good) over a super high heat, just brown enough to get some caramelisation – make sure the pan isn't overcrowded and avoid the pork sweating and stewing. Add the cumin, chilli powder, orange and lime juices, red wine vinegar, bay leaves, salt and pepper to the yumions. Stir and get it all hot.

3   At the same time, heat the stock in a saucepan to near boiling point. This will get the cooking started right away and lower the overall time of the braise.

4   Place all the seared pork back in your cast-iron casserole. Add the onion and spice mix, then add stock to cover. Throw in the orange rind. Cook in the oven, so that the internal temperature of the pot is about 80°C fan (180°F) and leave for 6–10 hours. It definitely won't be mush by then, especially if the temp never went too high.

5   When super tender and falling apart, remove the orange rind and bay leaves. Pull the pork apart using two forks and discard any lumps of fat. Line a rimmed baking sheet with foil and spread the pulled pork out in a single layer.

6   Increase the oven temperature to 'make crispy fast' (about 200°C fan/400°F).

7   Return the cast-iron casserole dish to the stove and bring the leftover liquid to the boil over a high heat. Boil for 10–15 minutes, until the liquid is thickened and glaze-y and delicious; when stirred, the spoon should leave a trail in the liquid. Drizzle the pork with the reduced cooking liquid. Place it all in the oven for 5 minutes or until the pork starts to brown and the edges become crispy. Remove the baking sheet from the oven and use a spatula to flip the pork pieces. Return to the oven for another 5 minutes, until the pork is browned and crispy (but not charred, unless that's your thing).

8   Allow to cool to room temperature before assembling the croissants. →

Dinner

TOMATO CHILLI JAM

1 kg (2 lb 4 oz) Roma tomatoes

8 long red chillies

6 garlic cloves

30 g (1 oz) fresh ginger, chopped

45 g (1½ oz) fish sauce

150 g (5 oz) red wine vinegar

450 g (1 lb) caster (superfine) sugar

1   Roughly chop half the tomatoes. Place the rest of the tomatoes in a blender with the chillies, garlic, ginger and fish sauce. Blend until smooth.

2   Combine the blended tomato mix, red wine vinegar and sugar in a large pot and bring to the boil, stirring to dissolve the sugar and skimming off any foam that forms on the surface. Once you have this at a rolling boil, add the roughly chopped tomatoes. Simmer over a low heat, stirring regularly, until the mixture has a thick, reduced, jammy consistency.

3   Allow to cool and store in a sealed container or sterilised jars in the fridge until required.

SHAPING

1   The Pulled Pork Croissants are shaped in the same manner as the Ham and Gruyère (page 49), with the filling placed on top of the stretched raw pastry then rolled up.

2   At the wide end of one of the croissants, spoon a heaped teaspoon of chilli jam and spread it out in a thin layer, covering the wide part of the triangle. On top of the chilli jam, place 20 g (¾ oz) of pulled pork. Finally, sprinkle 10 g (⅓ oz) of manchego and 10 g (⅓ oz) of queso fresco over the pulled pork.

3   Starting from the wide end of the triangle, and using your thumbs to keep the fillings in place, roll up the dough, finishing with the tip of the triangle on the underside of the croissant, and the 'ears' of the croissant touching your benchtop. Repeat for the remaining 4 croissants.

4   Evenly space the shaped pulled pork croissants on a baking tray, with enough space between each to allow for them to grow during the proving and baking process.

PROVING

1   Place your tray of shaped pulled pork croissants in your turned-off oven with a dish of boiling water in the bottom. Allow to prove for 5–6 hours, checking from the 5-hour mark, to ensure the croissants don't overprove. The pulled pork croissants are ready to bake when they are puffy, filled out, smooth, and more than doubled in size.

BAKING

1   Remove the tray of proven croissants and the dish of water from the oven. Preheat your oven to 210°C fan (410°F).

2   Using a soft-bristled pastry brush, carefully apply the egg wash, ensuring you don't use too much, to avoid egg pooling at the base of the croissant.

3   Bake the croissants for 5 minutes at 210°C fan (410°F), then knock your oven back to 160°C fan (320°F) and bake for a further 16 minutes. If you know your oven well and it has a hot spot, rotate your tray 180 degrees for the last 8 minutes.

4   Allow to cool for 10 minutes, then serve immediately with a guindilla pepper on a toothpick speared into the top of the pulled pork croissant.

Pour yourself a tequila, because you've just combined two incredibly diverse cuisines into one orgasmic culinary experience, and it's probably taken you at least four days to do so.

Fish Pie

6 ramekins, about 10 cm (4 in) diameter (internal)

850 g (1 lb 13 oz) croissant pastry scraps

1 egg, beaten ('egg wash')

green salad, to serve

fish pie filling

For nearly a decade now, the Builders Arms Hotel (BAH) in Fitzroy has been one of my favourite local haunts, setting the scene for everything from a regular solo Tuesday night burger, my 30th Birthday dinner party, to an infamous Lune staff Christmas party (never let me near a karaoke machine again). Safe to say, it's a Kate Reid favourite.

A few things haven't left the menu since Andrew McConnell assumed the role of custodian of the BAH, in particular, the ineffaceable Fish Pie.

The following Fish Pie appeared on the Lune Lab in August 2018, as my homage to the great BAH Fish Pie. The Lune Lab is an experience curated for eight lucky diners who are served up a three course degustation where we showcase our croissant pastry in creative and experimental courses. The menu changes every two months to reflect seasonality of produce, and also to keep our chefs engaged and innovating.

You'll also be thrilled to know that all those little scrap bits of pastry I've been asking you to save finally get a guernsey here! The beautiful little crispy, buttery spirals on top, and the slightly underbaked pastry where the saucy filling meets the pie lid make for one seriously perfect mouthful of food.

For the fish pie filling, the sauce is made first, the seafood added at the last minute, such that it does not overcook.

PASTRY SCRAP SWIRLS

1   Line a baking tray measuring no less than 35 × 25 cm (13¾ x 9¾ in) with baking paper.

2   If you have frozen the pastry scraps, transfer them to the fridge the night before before you plan to serve the fish pies. The next day, trim them such that they are all about 5 mm (¼ in) in width then create little spirals with each piece of pastry and place them on the lined baking tray, making sure the cut side exposing the lamination is facing up. Repeat this until you have filled the baking tray, spirals touching each other and nestled in closely, as you want them to prove and bake into each other. Once you have filled a tray with spirals, store in the fridge until you are ready to prove them.

3   About 3 hours before you plan to serve dinner, place the tray of spirals in your turned-off oven with a dish of boiling water in the bottom of the oven, and prove for about 2 hours, until the spirals start to puff up, filling in the little gaps between each spiral.

4   Remove the tray of proven spirals and dish of water from the oven and place the tray of spirals, uncovered, in the fridge. →

FISH PIE FILLING

80 g (2¾ oz) butter

10 g (⅓ oz) extra virgin olive oil

100 g (3½ oz) leek, finely chopped

80 g (2¾ oz) fennel,
finely chopped

1 garlic clove, finely chopped

sea salt, to taste

freshly ground black pepper,
to taste

pinch of cayenne pepper

550 g (1 lb 3 oz) milk

60 g (2 oz) white wine

75 g (2½ oz) plain (all-purpose)
flour, sifted

5 g (0.2 oz) Dijon mustard

70 g (2½ oz) thickened cream

grated zest of ½ lemon

1 tablespoon finely chopped dill

2 tablespoons finely
chopped sorrel

200 g (7 oz) skinless ocean/
sea trout fillet, cut into 1.5 cm
(½ in) pieces

200 g (7 oz) Spanish mackerel,
cut into 1.5 cm (½ in) pieces

50 g (1¾ oz) raw prawn meat,
cut into 1 cm (½ in) pieces

1 tablespoon capers,
roughly chopped

1 Heat the butter and olive oil in a medium saucepan over a low heat. Once the butter is melted, add the leek, fennel and garlic and sauté until they are soft and translucent. Season with salt, black pepper and the cayenne pepper.

2 Meanwhile, in another small saucepan, heat the milk, bringing it almost to the boil.

3 Deglaze the pan of leek, fennel and garlic with the white wine and cook out the alcohol in the wine for 2–3 minutes, then add the flour and stir well, cooking the adapted roux for 2–3 minutes. Continuing to stir the roux, begin to pour in the warmed milk. Once all the milk is added, bring the béchamel to a gentle boil and allow to boil for 1 minute, stirring continuously, until it thickens slightly. Remove from the heat and finally stir in the Dijon mustard, thickened cream, lemon zest, dill and sorrel.

4 Let the sauce cool before gently folding through the fish and prawn mixture and the capers, then divide the mixture evenly between the 6 ramekins.

ASSEMBLING AND BAKING

1 Preheat the oven to 160°C fan (320°F).

2 Take the tray of proven, chilled pastry spirals from the fridge.

3 Using a cutter that is just a tiny bit smaller than the internal diameter of the ramekin, carefully cut a round of proven pastry from the tray, ensuring that where you have placed the cutter on the tray will allow for 5 other full rounds to be cut. While the cutter is still in situ, gently slide a spatula or flat egg slide underneath the cut pastry and place it carefully on top of the fish pie filling in a ramekin. If you have chosen the correct sized cutter, the pastry spirals should sit snuggly in the ramekin, atop the pie filling. Repeat this process to cut the pastry 'tops' for each of the individual fish pies.

4 When the 6 ramekins are complete with their fish pie fillings and proven pastry spiral tops, using a soft bristled brush, carefully egg-wash the pastry spiral tops.

5 Load the 6 ramekins onto a large tray and place in the preheated oven for 20 minutes, until the pastry spirals are golden and the sauce is starting to bubble up around the edges.

6 Remove from the oven and rest for 10 minutes before serving.

CHEF NOTE The sauce for the fish pie is a slightly more complex version of a béchamel, using the same technique of creating a roux, then adding milk.

Tomato and Taleggio Danish

YIELDS 6

6 blind-baked danishes
(page 93)

Taleggio bechamel

roasted mini Roma tomatoes

black garlic croissant crumb

sherry glaze

Over a bowl of carbonara one night, my good friend and MasterChef Australia judge, Jock Zonfrillo, proposed a JZ-inspired Lune pastry; a smoked tomato and Taleggio number. I took the idea straight to my Head Chef in Fitzroy, who immediately set about developing the pastry. The result was a multi-layered, complex, mouth-wateringly delicious danish, that earned the Zonfrillo seal of approval.

At Lune we smoked the tomatoes over woodchips, but for this recipe I have omitted the smoking – you still get exceptional flavour from the tomatoes through caramelisation in the pan.

As per the Danish recipes in the Morning Tea chapter, this one is blind baked, so follow the same proving and baking instructions on pages 83 and 93.

BLACK GARLIC CROISSANT CRUMB

2 black garlic bulbs

1 day-old croissant

grated zest of ½ orange
(about 1 teaspoon)

sea salt

1   Preheat your oven to 80°C fan (180°F).

2   Squeeze the black garlic out of the bulbs onto a baking tray lined with baking paper. Using a palette knife, spread the garlic as thinly as possible. Dehydrate (dry out) the black garlic in the oven for several hours.

3   Preheat your oven to 160°C fan (320°F).

4   Tear the day-old croissant into bite-size pieces, place on a baking tray and bake for about 10 minutes, until the pieces are crispy and have taken on a golden brown colour all over. Take out of the oven and cool to room temperature.

5   Place the dehydrated black garlic, the cooled croissant pieces and the orange zest in a blender or food processor and blitz until you have a fine crumb. For the crunchiest results, prepare the crumb the same day you plan to serve the danishes. The crumb will keep in an airtight container for a couple of days but will lose a little of its freshness after the first day.

ROASTED MINI ROMA TOMATOES

about 100 g (3½ oz) caster (superfine) sugar

olive oil

500 g (1 lb 3 oz) mini Roma tomatoes, halved

1   Put the caster (superfine) sugar in a small bowl.

2   Coat the base of a frying pan in olive oil and warm over a medium heat. Carefully dip the cut side of the tomatoes in the sugar, then place the tomatoes, sugary cut side down, in the pan. Allow the tomatoes to cook for a minute or two – long enough to begin to caramelise – checking their level of doneness by carefully lifting a tomato half with tongs every 30 seconds or so. When they are ready they will have taken on colour and look a little crinkly, like the beginnings of a semi-sundried tomato. If you wanted to introduce a little bit of smokiness, you could carry out this process on the hotplate of a barbecue.

3   Allow the tomatoes to cool to room temperature. If you have prepared the tomatoes a day in advance, carefully store, cut side up, in a sealed container in the fridge – you want to maintain the shape and integrity of the tomato halves. →

TALEGGIO BÉCHAMEL

30 g (1 oz) butter

½ shallot, finely chopped

240 g (8½ oz) milk

30 g (1 oz) flour

90 g (3¼ oz) Taleggio, rind removed, chopped

salt and pepper, to taste

1   Melt the butter in a small saucepan over a medium heat, add the shallot and sauté until soft and translucent.

2   In another saucepan, bring the milk to a simmer, then remove immediately from heat.

3   Add the flour to the melted butter and shallot and stir continuously with a whisk until fully combined. Cook the roux over a medium heat for a couple of minutes, stirring, until it just starts to catch on the bottom of the pan and becomes blonde in colour.

4   While continuing to whisk the roux, begin to pour in the warmed milk. Once all the milk is added, bring the béchamel to a gentle boil and allow to boil for 1 minute, stirring continuously.

5   Take off the heat and add the Taleggio, stirring to fully combine. Finally, season to taste. Allow to cool to room temperature. Transfer to a piping bag if you like, though this isn't essential.

SHERRY GLAZE

100 g (3½ oz) sherry vinegar

20 g (¾ oz) caster (superfine) sugar

10 g (⅓ oz) balsamic vinegar

pinch of sea salt

1   Put the sherry vinegar and sugar in a small saucepan over a medium heat and reduce until it coats the back of a spoon. Add the balsamic vinegar and salt and stir to combine.

FINISHING

1   Ensure that before assembling you have allowed the tomatoes to come to room temperature. If you have made them in advance and stored in the fridge, bring them out of the fridge about 1 hour before you plan to serve the danishes.

2   Take your 6 cooled, unfilled blind-baked danish shells. Brush all of the outside of the danishes with the warmed sherry glaze (do not brush inside the cavity where you will assemble the fillings).

3   Pipe a thick layer of the Taleggio béchamel into each danish shell, approximately 40 g (1½ oz). If your béchamel isn't in a piping bag, you can just spoon it in, using a palette knife to spread the béchamel all the way into the corners of the danish.

4   Nestle 9 caramelised tomato halves on top of the béchamel, overlapping them so that they are sitting proud of the danish shell.

5   Finally sprinkle some black garlic crumb over the tomatoes.
Serve immediately.

Thanks, Jock.

Blind-Baked Croissants

YIELDS 5

5 standard cannoli tubes (18–20 cm/7–8 in in diameter), buttered and wrapped in baking paper

1 batch of pastry, rolled out and cut for croissants

1 egg, beaten ('egg wash')

After we realised that blind-baking danishes provided us with the perfect blank canvas for an infinite number of flavour combinations and fillings, we started playing around with blind-baking other pastry shapes, and we landed on this absolute gem.

The blind-baked croissant.

I often think that the traditional croissant is the best way to showcase the perfect lamination of our pastry, and it's also *such* a pleasing pastry to eat, due not only to the beautiful celebration of butter, but also the textural variation in the architecture of the pastry itself. There are crunchy bits, chewy bits, light-as-a-cloud bits; I will never get bored of eating a good plain croissant.

One thing that absolutely gets my goat is the way many cafes, the world over, simply hack a plain croissant in half and shove things inside it (and often then squash it in a sandwich press! I mean, what an *abomination*!), completely destroying the magnificent architecture of that honeycomb interior that took three days to construct!

I do have to admit that sometimes (*sometimes*) it's actually quite nice to eat a plain croissant with other ingredients, but how do you do that without simply cutting one in half?

Answer: you bake a hole in the centre of it. Enter an entirely new croissant vehicle, destined to carry whatever delicious filling us Lune chefs can dream up! In the following pages, I've been kind enough to share three of our top fillings for blind-baked croissants.

Once you've mastered the blind bake, feel free to go rogue and fill your croissants with whatever deliciousness your heart desires!

SHAPE AS PER HAM AND GRUYERE WITH THE BELOW VARIATION SEE PAGE 49

1 Place one prepared cannoli tube at the wide end of the triangle, about 1 cm (½ in) below the small nick in the centre.

2 Starting from the wide end of the triangle, gently pull the nick apart and over the top of the cannoli tube. Using your thumbs to keep the tube in place, roll the pastry up, finishing with the tip of the triangle on the underside, and the 'ears' of the croissant touching your benchtop. Place the shaped croissants on a baking tray, well spaced to allow them to expand during the proving and baking process.

PROVE AS PER HAM AND GRUYERE SEE PAGE 50

SHAPE AS PER HAM AND GRUYERE WITH THE BELOW VARIATION SEE PAGE 50

1 Using oven mitts, carefully remove the cannoli tubes as soon as the croissants are taken out of the oven.

2 Allow to cool for at least 10 minutes before filling and serving.

Dinner

Boeuf Bourguignon

6 blind-baked croissants

beef bourguignon

mashed potato

kale chips

shaved truffle, to serve

salt and pepper, to season

What's better than one French icon? Two, of course. Put croissant and boeuf bourguignon in not just the same sentence, but also the same mouthful, and the result is something far greater than the sum of its already pretty great parts.

BEEF BOURGUIGNON

olive oil, for cooking

2 brown onions, diced

3 garlic cloves, finely chopped

220 g (7¾ oz) mushrooms, thinly sliced

5 carrots, cut into 1 cm (½ in) dice

5 slices of bacon, finely chopped

1.3 kg (2 lbs 14 oz) boneless beef chuck, cut into 2 cm (¾ in) cubes

250 g (9 oz/1 cup) red wine

500g (1 lb 2 oz/2 cups) chicken stock

90 g (3¼ oz/½ cup) tomato paste

60 g (2 oz/¼ cup) soy sauce

40 g (1½ oz) plain (all-purpose) flour

2 tablespoons fresh thyme leaves, finely chopped

1   Preheat your oven to 175°C fan (350°F).

2   Heat some olive oil in a large cast-iron casserole dish or Dutch oven over a medium heat, add the onion and garlic and sweat until translucent. Add the mushrooms and cook for 10 minutes, then add the carrots and cook for a further 10 minutes, stirring often. Using a slotted spoon, temporarily transfer the vegetables to a bowl while you prepare the rest of the ingredients.

3   In the same casserole dish, cook the bacon over a medium heat. Once sizzling and starting to crisp, transfer the bacon to the same bowl with the onion and carrots using a slotted spoon.

4   Season the beef well and add some of it to the casserole dish, searing on each side for 2–3 minutes over medium-high heat. Do this in small batches; you don't want to overcrowd the dish; you want the beef to brown and caramelise a little on the outside, not stew. Transfer cooked batches of beef to a plate.

5   Once all the beef is seared, add the red wine to deglaze the casserole dish, scraping any little caramelised bits off the base and sides of the dish. Allow the red wine to reduce slightly, then add the chicken stock, tomato paste and soy sauce. Add the flour and whisk to combine. Put all the other prepared ingredients back into the casserole dish, including the fresh thyme, give it a good stir, pop the lid on and transfer to the oven. Allow the boeuf bourguignon to cook for 1½–2 hours, until the beef is so tender that it's falling apart. At the 1-hour mark, check the stew and stir gently to ensure that the beef isn't drying out.

6   If you have prepared the beef a day in advance, transfer to a sealed container and store in the fridge.

MASHED POTATO

rock salt

500 g (1 lb 2 oz) red potatoes, washed, skin on

125 g (4½ oz) thickened cream

50 g (1¾ oz) butter

1   For this mashed potato recipe, the potatoes are cooked in the oven, rather than boiled.

2   Preheat your oven to 180°C fan (350°F).

3   Completely cover a baking tray with rock salt then lay the washed potatoes, whole, on top of the salt. The salt will help to draw moisture out of the potatoes. Roast the potatoes for 1–½ hours (the time will vary based on the size of the potatoes: obviously, the bigger the potato, the longer the cooking time). The potatoes are ready when a paring knife glides effortlessly into the potato. Remove from the oven, cut the potatoes in half and carefully scoop the flesh out of the skin.

4   Place a fine drum sieve over a bowl and, using a pastry scraper, pass the potato flesh through the sieve. Transfer the potato to a saucepan, add the cream and butter and mix over a low heat, until the mash is smooth and creamy. Season to taste with salt and pepper. →

KALE CHIPS

1 bunch of kale

1 Preheat the oven to 100°C fan (210°F) and line baking trays with baking paper.

2 Bring a large saucepan of water to the boil and prepare an ice bath in a large bowl.

3 Carefully cut the kale leaves off their stalks by running a paring knife up each side of the stalk. Wash the leaves well, then blanch them in the boiling water for 2 minutes, transferring them immediately from the pan to the ice bath to stop them cooking, allowing the kale to retain its colour.

4 Pat the leaves dry thoroughly in paper towel. Any residual water will reduce the crispiness of the kale chips (and frankly no one wants that).

5 Place the blanched, dried kale leaves in a single layer on the lined baking trays, being careful not to overcrowd the kale – it requires the air around it to crisp up nicely. Season generously with salt and bake for 45–60 minutes, until dried and crispy.

FINISHING

1 Just before serving, warm the boeuf bourguignon in a small saucepan and transfer into a piping bag.

2 As per the beef, if the mashed potato has been made in advance, warm the potato in a small saucepan just before service. Spoon a generous amount of mash onto each plate, making a little crater in the mash with the back of a dessert spoon.

3 Cut a hole in the tip of a piping bag of boeuf bourguignon, about 1 cm (½ in) (enough for the beef to fit through the opening), then take a blind-baked croissant and pipe a generous amount of beef into each open end of the croissant. The croissant should feel significantly heavier! (Alternatively, you can just spoon the beef straight into the cavity of the blind-baked croissant).

4 Place the croissant to one side of the mash, garnish with a few kale chips, then finish the dish off with some truffle shavings.

5 Repeat with all the croissants and serve immediately.

Fried Chicken Croissant

YIELDS 5

5 blind-baked croissants, garnished with a pinch of sweet paprika on top pre-bake

chicken tenders

vegetable oil, for deep frying

Nashville hot sauce

Kewpie mayo, coleslaw and dill pickles, to serve

Many moons ago we teamed up with our mates at Belles Hot Chicken in Fitzroy for one incredibly fun night to bring the people of Melbourne the notorious 'Double Down'; two fried chicken tenders and some appropriately soothing condiments, served in a traditional croissant.

With the advent of the blind-baked croissant, we decided to develop a fried chicken croissant, inspired by the Double Down but reimagined for Lune Lab.

This thing will be the best fried chicken burger you've ever had.

DILL PICKLES

1 kg (2 lb 4 oz) baby cucumbers

85 g (3 oz) flaked sea salt

10 g (⅓ oz) black peppercorns

10 g (⅓ oz) coriander seeds

10 g (⅓ oz) yellow mustard seeds

2 bay leaves

700 g (1 lb 9 oz) white wine vinegar

100 g (3½ oz) caster (superfine) sugar

a handful of dill sprigs

PREPARE AT LEAST TWO WEEKS IN ADVANCE

1 Place the whole baby cucumbers in a large bowl and cover them with the salt, tossing well. Cover the bowl with cling film and leave overnight.

2 The next day the salt will have drawn out liquid from the cucumbers, creating a brine with the salt. The cucumbers will still feel a little gritty from salt that hasn't fully dissolved. Drain the brine, putting 100 g (3½ oz) aside for the chicken marinade and transferring the rest into a saucepan.

3 Toast the spices in a dry frying pan over a high heat until aromatic.

4 Add the bay leaves, white wine vinegar and caster (superfine) sugar to the saucepan with the brine and bring to the boil, stirring to dissolve the sugar.

5 Transfer the cucumbers into sterilised jars, making sure that they are packed in tight, and add some sprigs of dill. Pour the hot pickling liquid into the jars, making sure to completely cover the cucumbers. Allow to cool completely to room temperature, seal with lids then transfer to the fridge.

CHICKEN TENDERS

500 g (1 lb 2 oz) chicken tenderloins

400 g (14 oz) buttermilk

100 g (3½ oz) dill pickle brine (above)

2 eggs, lightly beaten

PREPARE A DAY IN ADVANCE

1 Trim the chicken tenders, such that they will fit through the hole in the croissant (no more than 2 cm/¾ in at their widest point) and lay them in a shallow baking dish.

2 Place the buttermilk, dill pickle brine and eggs in a bowl and whisk to combine. Pour the marinade over the chicken, cover the dish with cling film and transfer to the fridge for 24 hours.

NASHVILLE HOT SAUCE

115 g (4 oz) clarified butter (see page 10) or ghee

20 g (¾ oz) brown sugar

30 g (1 oz) cayenne pepper

10 g (⅓ oz) smoked paprika

3 g (0.1 oz) garlic powder

1 Place the clarified butter in a small saucepan over a medium heat and re-melt. Add the remaining hot sauce ingredients to the liquid clarified butter and whisk for 1 minute over a low heat until emulsified. Cool then store in the fridge. →

CHEF NOTE If you are using unclarified butter for the sauce, start with 150 g (5 oz) of butter and clarify as per the instructions on page 10.

BUTTERMILK COLESLAW

300 g (10½ oz) thinly shredded cabbage (mix of white and purple)

½ red onion, thinly sliced

1 carrot, peeled and coarsely grated

30 g (1 oz) Kewpie mayonnaise

90 g (3¼ oz) buttermilk

1 teaspoon Dijon mustard

1 teaspoon apple cider vinegar

5 g (0.2 oz) caster (superfine) sugar

1 Combine the cabbage, onion and carrot in a large bowl and season, tossing well to mix. In another bowl, whisk together the remaining ingredients to make the dressing. Pour the dressing over the shredded cabbage mix and toss well to coat. Taste to check the seasoning and refrigerate until ready to serve.

SPICED DRY MIX FOR THE CHICKEN

400 g (14 oz) plain (all-purpose) flour

200 g (7 oz) cornflour (cornstarch)

20 g (¾ oz) garlic powder

30 g (1 oz) onion powder

20 g (¾ oz) sweet paprika

20 g (¾ oz) hot paprika

10 g (⅓ oz) cayenne pepper

1 Sift all the ingredients into a large bowl to remove any lumps, and whisk to fully combine dry ingredients, getting a good distribution of spices throughout the flour.

FINISHING

1 Remove the marinated chicken from the fridge 30 minutes before you plan to fry it.

2 Fill a high-sided pot at least 8 cm (3 in) deep with oil and heat the oil to 180°C fan (350°F) (use a thermometer to monitor the temperature).

3 Once the oil is at temperature, remove the chicken from the marinade and dust each tender in the spiced dry mix, shaking off any excess clumps - the aim is a light dusting, not a heavy batter. I would recommend prepping all your chicken tenders before beginning to deep fry.

4 In small batches, depending on the size of your pot, deep-fry 3–4 chicken tenders at a time. Fry the tenders for 6–7 minutes then remove with a slotted spoon and drain on paper towel. After you have removed your first batch of tenders, use a thermometer to check one for an internal temperature of at least 70°C fan (160°F).

5 Meanwhile, re-melt the hot sauce in a saucepan. As soon as the tenders are ready, brush them with a little of the warmed Nashville hot sauce.

6 To serve, carefully slide a tender into the centre of each croissant, then squeeze a little Kewpie mayonnaise into each open end of the croissant.

7 Place a little mound of coleslaw on each plate, off centre. Cut several pickles in half lengthways, then top the coleslaw with 2 halves of pickle.

8 Plate a fried chicken croissant on each serving plate, next to the coleslaw.

You will have extra chicken tenders, but I don't know anyone that's ever stopped at one tender … Consider serving the rest on a platter with the coleslaw, so that your guests can continue to graze to their heart's content.

Lobster 'Rolls'

YIELDS 6

2 lobster tails, cooked, meat removed from shell

1 avocado, diced

mayonnaise

1 bunch of chives, chopped

baby cos lettuce leaves, roughly chopped

1 bunch of dill, fronds picked

vinaigrette

6 blind-baked croissants

A lobster roll is classically prepared with a long brioche bun. It feels entirely appropriate to me to take it to the next level and serve it with a croissant instead.

MAYONNAISE

4 egg yolks

25 g (1 oz) hot English mustard

10 g (⅓ oz) Dijon mustard

5 g (0.2 oz) wholegrain mustard

1 tablespoon white wine vinegar

1 teaspoon lemon juice

1 confit garlic clove

pinch of salt

375 g (13 oz) canola oil (or any neutral oil)

1–2 tablespoons hot water

1   Place the egg yolks, mustards, vinegar, lemon juice, garlic and salt in a food processor and blend to combine.

2   While the food processor is running, add the oil in a slow and steady stream. It will begin to thicken when half the oil has been added.

3   At this stage, add 1 tablespoon of the hot water. Continue to drizzle in the remaining oil with the food processor motor still running.

4   Once all the oil has been added, if the consistency is still too thick, add more hot water to obtain a thinner mayonnaise, remembering that in this application it will be used to lightly dress the lobster, so you are looking for more of a dressing consistency rather than a classic mayonnaise.

5   Transfer to a container and reserve in the fridge until required.

VINAIGRETTE

100 g (3½ oz) sherry vinegar

50 g (1¾ oz) lemon juice

15 g (½ oz) sea salt flakes

350 g (12 oz) olive oil (extra virgin is recommended)

black pepper, to taste

1   Weigh everything into a bowl except for the olive oil, then drizzle in the oil in a slow, steady stream, emulsifying the vinaigrette by whisking constantly until all the olive oil has been added in. Taste the vinaigrette and check the seasoning, adding salt and pepper to taste. Set aside until required.

FINISHING

1   Dice the lobster meat into 1 cm (½ in) pieces and transfer to a bowl with the avocado then stir in the mayonnaise and seasoning. Sprinkle with chives.

2   Lightly toss the leaves and dill fronds in vinaigrette and season.

3   Place a couple of the pieces of chopped lettuce inside each croissant, making sure that they poke out of the ends a little – the lettuce will act both as a garnish and a scoop to hold any lobster filling that may spill out.

4   Carefully spoon a generous amount of the dressed lobster into both ends of each of the croissants, ensuring that the lobster goes all the way to the middle. Serve immediately!

Dinner

Dessert

In August 2014 Cam and I went to see the old warehouse in Fitzroy. As big as a basketball court (at least 20 times the size of the shop in Elwood), tucked away down a narrow one-way residential street, the turn-of-the-century building had a bit of a 'secret lair' vibe about it, reminiscent of the *Oceans 11* disused warehouse at the docks, where criminal masterminds constructed the perfect replica of a bank vault. Although it was *so much bigger* than we needed, we both saw the vision.

As it would be near impossible to climate control such a huge space, especially given the age of the building, we imagined a room right in the centre. A room made of glass, such that the customers could see the pastry chefs lovingly labouring over the croissants, but the pastry chefs could also witness the customers enjoying their spoils. The space would be laboratory like, each surface spotless, clinical, advocating attention to detail and perfection, in complete juxtaposition to the surrounding timeworn brick walls that had bore witness to varying operations over the past century.

We both imagined passers by doing a double take when, out of the corner of their eye, they spied this unlikely scene.

The concept was so *un-bakery*. It flipped the traditional layout of a food business on its head. The space would be constructed with a priority focus on the perfect environment and workflow for croissant production. It would be unapologetically designed for function. But, inadvertently, when you create a space with the experience of the user front of mind, you typically end up with beautiful form, because to witness people working in an environment conceived exclusively for them, is to witness a choreographed dance, every move necessary and intended and in unison with their fellow dancers. If you have had the pleasure of sitting opposite the *Cube* at Lune, you will know exactly what I'm talking about.

Lune opened its Headquarters in Fitzroy in October 2015.

Pear Tarte Tatin

YIELDS 6

6 springform tins,
11 cm (4½ in) in diameter

1 batch of pastry, rolled out to
32 × 24 cm (12½ x 9½ in)

softened butter, to grease

caster (superfine) sugar,
to dust

sea salt flakes, to scatter

poached pears

pear caramel

vanilla bean ice cream, to serve

There is nothing quite like that 'hot and cold' combination when it comes to food, in particular when the cold element is velvety and rich, a coating for your mouth of soothing, just melted, yet still cool, ice cream.

The real beauty of this dish is you can serve it literally straight from the oven, piping hot; the caramel still a gorgeous deep golden bubbling liquid. As soon as that scoop of ice cream is placed atop the tarte tatin, it begins its delicious transformation from frozen sphere to, moment by moment, puddle of rich, melted, cool vanilla cream, that slowly works its way into all the little nooks and crannies of pear and pastry.

For this recipe I would recommend using a variety of pear that is still firm when it is ripe, such as beurre bosc or conference pears. The pears get cooked twice, first poached, then in the oven, and let's be honest, no one likes a mushy pear.

POACHED PEARS

1 kg (2 lb 4 oz) caster (superfine) sugar

850 g (1 lb 13 oz) water

650 g (1 lb 7 oz) white wine

1 lemon, quartered

1 vanilla pod, seeds scraped

1 star anise

2 cinnamon sticks

1 kg (2 lb 4 oz) firm pears, peeled, quartered and cored

1   Bring the sugar, water and wine to the boil in a large pan over a high heat, then add the lemon, vanilla and star anise and cinnamon sticks.

2   Add the pear quarters to the simmering poaching syrup and place a cartouche on the surface of the syrup to keep the pears submerged at all times. Poach over a low heat for 10–15 minutes, keeping a close eye on them so they don't overcook (remember they will be cooked again in the oven, so it is preferable that they are slightly undercooked at this stage rather than over). The pears are ready when a paring knife pierces the flesh of the pear with no resistance.

3   Remove the pears with a slotted spoon and transfer them to a large shallow container. Allow the poaching liquid to cool completely to room temperature, then cover the pear halves in cooled syrup and store in the fridge until required.

PEAR CARAMEL

600 g (1 lb 5 oz) caster (superfine) sugar

1 teaspoon ground cinnamon

1 teaspoon mixed spice

75 g (2½ oz) poaching liquid

10 g (⅓ oz) vanilla extract

1   Put a clean, dry saucepan over a medium heat. Once the pan is hot, gradually sprinkle in some of the sugar, wait for it to melt, then sprinkle in a little more, waiting each time until all the sugar is melted before adding more. Once the sugar is melted and evenly caramelised, reaching a light amber colour, remove from the heat and add the spices.

2   Slowly and progressively add the poaching liquid, whisking vigorously after each addition to avoid the caramel seizing. Once all the poaching liquid has been added whisk to combine then remove from the heat.

3   Set aside until ready to use.

PREPARING THE PASTRY DISCS

1   Using a 10 cm (4 in) cutter, cut 6 discs from the sheet of croissant pastry. Transfer them to a tray lined with baking paper and reserve in the fridge until ready to assemble the tarte tatins. →

Dessert

TIN PREPARATION

1   Brush the springform tins with a liberal amount of softened butter, line the base of the tins with a disc of baking paper, then butter the upside of the baking paper too. Pour a tablespoon of sugar into each tin and toss around to coat the base and sides evenly. Finally, sprinkle a large pinch of sea salt flakes over the base of each tin. Place the tins on a baking tray and set aside.

ASSEMBLING

1   Pour 35 g (1¼ oz) of caramel into the base of each prepared tin.

2   Next, prepare the pears. Remove 2 quarters of pear per tarte tatin, so 12 quarters in total. Drain the poached quarters on absorbent paper to soak up any excess poaching liquid. Cut each quarter lengthways into thin slices, about 2 mm thick.

3   Taking the slices from 2 pear quarters, fan them out in a circular fashion, then lay the circle of pear slices on top of the caramel in the base of one prepared tin. Repeat for all the prepared tins.

4   Finally, lay a pastry disc on top of the pear slices.

PROVING

1   Arrange the 6 tins on a baking tray and place the tray in a turned-off oven with a dish of hot water in the bottom. Prove for 5–6 hours, until the disc of pastry is puffy, shiny, and touching the edges of the tin.

BAKING

1   Remove the tray of proven tarte tatins from the oven as well as the dish of water, then preheat your oven to 210°C fan (410°F).

2   Once your oven is at temperature, load the tray of tarte tatins into the oven and bake for 5 minutes at 210°C fan (410°F), then reduce the temperature to 160°C fan (320°F) and bake for a further 10–12 minutes, until the pastry is a deep golden brown and the caramel is bubbling up the sides of the tin.

3   Remove from the oven, and, using oven mitts, immediately invert the tins onto individual serving plates; if you leave them to cool in the tin for even a short amount of time the caramel will harden and stick.

4   Serve with a scoop of the best quality vanilla bean ice cream you can source, dolloped right in the centre of each bubbling-hot tarte tatin.

Paris-Brest

YIELDS 6

hazelnut parfait

300 g (10½ oz) double
(heavy) cream, whipped

chocolate and hazelnut
ganache

Dulce de Leche,
prepared a day in advance
(Essentials, see page 264)

hazelnut praline

candied hazelnuts

This recipe uses an adapted kouign-amann, rather than the
characteristic choux pastry ring, to form the pastry base of this
classic French dessert which is shaped as a ring to represent
a bicycle wheel, a nod to the infamous bicycle race held each
year between Paris and Brest.
    This recipe is rich, decadent, indulgent, and generous,
so I would recommend serving it following a light main course!
    Praline paste can be found at most specialty ingredient stores.

SHAPING

6 springform tins (rings only),
11 cm (4½ in) in diameter, greased
and lined with baking paper

3 cm (1¼ in) cutter

6 food-safe metal rings,
greased and lined with baking
paper around the outside

1 batch of pastry, rolled out
and cut for kouign-amann
(escargot)

100 g (3½ oz) softened butter

caster (superfine) sugar

sea salt flakes

1   Arrange the prepared rings on a baking tray lined with baking paper.

2   Brush the softened butter evenly across the 6 strips of pastry.
Now sprinkle an even blanket of caster sugar over the butter, leaving the
last 3 cm (1¼ in) unsugared for each strip. Using your index finger, gently
spread the sugar for even distribution.

3   Roll the first strip gently towards yourself, creating little to no tension
as you go. Now carefully pick up the tight spiral and dip both the top
and bottom surfaces in the reserved sugar, then place in the centre of
a prepared ring. Repeat for the remaining strips of pastry.

4   Place the baking tray with the shaped kouign-amann in the fridge until
you are ready to begin proving.

PROVING

1   Place your tray of KAs in your turned-off oven with a dish of boiling
water in the bottom and allow to prove for 5–6 hours. They are ready
when they are at least doubled in size, and touching the sides of the rings.

BAKING

1   Remove the tray of proven KAs from oven and transfer them to the fridge
for 20–30 minutes, until firm to touch.

2   Meanwhile, remove the dish of water from the bottom of the oven
and turn the oven on to 210°C fan (410°F).

3   Once the KAs have firmed up, using the 3 cm (1¼ in) cutter, cut the
centre out of each of the kouign-amann and put a lined 3 cm (1¼ in) ring in
the middle. Put a piece of baking paper over the top of the 6 proven KAs,
then a weighted tray, to keep the tops flat as they rise in the oven.

4   Load into the preheated oven and bake for 5 minutes, then knock your
oven back to 160°C fan (320°F) and bake for a further 16 minutes.

5   Once the 16-minute cycle has finished, take the pastries out of the oven
then, using oven mitts, carefully remove the top tray, the springform rings
and the 3 cm (1¼ in) internal rings, then load the kouign-amann 'rings' back
into the oven for 5 minutes, until they are golden and caramelised.

6   Allow to cool completely. →

Dessert

HAZELNUT PRALINE

250 g (9 oz) hazelnuts

500 g (1 lb 2 oz) sugar

50 g (1¾ oz) water

50 g (1¾ oz) butter

5 g (0.2 oz) salt

1   Preheat the oven to 170°C fan (340°F).

2   Place the hazelnuts on a baking tray and roast for about 10 minutes, until golden brown.

3   Meanwhile, place the sugar and water in a saucepan over a medium heat and bring to the boil, cooking until the sugar has caramelised and has taken on a dark caramel colour. Carefully add the butter and salt, whisking to emulsify the butter into the caramel.

4   Add the roasted hazelnuts, stirring them through the caramel with a heatproof spoon or spatula, such that they are completely coated in the caramel. Tip the coated hazelnuts onto a lined baking tray and allow to cool completely to room temperature.

5   Once the candied hazelnuts have cooled completely, break up into chunks and, in a food processor, blitz in small batches to a rough praline crumb, but not quite a powder. Store in an airtight container.

HAZELNUT PARFAIT

300 g (10½ oz) thickened cream

35 g (1¼ oz) praline paste

120 g (4¼ oz) caster (superfine) sugar

6 egg yolks

45 g (1½ oz) water

1 gold-strength gelatine leaf, soaked in cold water

90 g (3¼ oz) hazelnut praline

1   Grease and line a deep-sided tray (about 30 × 20 cm/12 × 8 in) with baking paper.

2   In the bowl of a stand mixer fitted with the whisk attachment whip the thickened cream and praline paste together until soft peaks form then transfer to a clean bowl and set aside in the fridge.

3   Place the egg yolks and 40 g (1½ oz) of the caster (superfine) sugar in the bowl of the stand mixer and, again using the whisk attachment, whip until pale and fluffy.

4   Meanwhile, bring the remaining 80 g (2¾ oz) of sugar and the water to the boil in a small saucepan over a medium heat. Monitor the temperature using a sugar thermometer and take off the heat when the syrup reaches 110°C fan (230°F).

5   Add the soaked gelatine leaf to the hot syrup, whisk to dissolve, then slowly and carefully pour the sugar syrup into the eggs while they are still whisking. Once all the syrup is added, continue to whisk until the bowl feels like skin temperature.

6   Take the cream from the fridge and add about one quarter of the whipped cream to the eggs, folding in gently to combine. Fold through the remaining cream then reserve in the fridge for 10 minutes.

7   Once the parfait has firmed up slightly, sprinkle in the hazelnut praline crumbs and fold through gently. Transfer to the prepared tray, spreading the parfait as evenly as possible in the tray, then give the tray a gentle tap on the benchtop to ensure that it is totally flat. Cover the tray with foil and transfer to the freezer to allow to set completely.

8   Once the parfait is set completely, remove from the freezer and carefully turn it out of the tray onto a chopping board. Working quickly, using a 10 cm (4 in) cutter, cut 6 discs from the slab of parfait, then cut a 3 cm (1¼ in) hole out of the middle of each. Transfer the frozen rings of parfait to a shallow container lined with baking paper and return them to the freezer.

CHOCOLATE AND HAZELNUT GANACHE

150 g (5 oz) thickened cream

pinch of salt

50 g (1¾ oz) hazelnut praline paste

150 g (5 oz) milk chocolate

20 g (¾ oz) butter, room temperature

1 Place the cream, salt and praline paste in a small saucepan and bring to just before the boil while whisking, to avoid the praline paste catching.

2 Meanwhile, weigh the milk chocolate and butter into a small heatproof bowl.

3 Pour the hot cream over the milk and butter, whisking to melt and combine the chocolate and cream.

4 Allow to come completely to room temperature then cover the bowl with cling film and leave overnight for the ganache to set.

5 The following day transfer the ganache into a piping bag.

CANDIED HAZELNUTS

250 g (9 oz) hazelnuts

vegetable oil, for deep frying

75 g (2½ oz) water

125 g (4½ oz) caster (superfine) sugar

sea salt flakes

1 Preheat the oven to 170°C fan (340°F).

2 Using a sharp knife, carefully cut the hazelnuts in half down the natural split. Once all the nuts have been halved, transfer to a baking tray and roast the nuts for 10 minutes.

3 Half-fill a medium saucepan with vegetable oil and bring to 'deep fry' temperature (about 180°C fan/350°F).

4 In another small saucepan bring the water and sugar to the boil. Add the halved roasted hazelnuts and, using a sugar thermometer, leave the nuts to cook until the syrup reaches 110°C fan (230°F). As soon as this temperature is reached, strain the nuts out of the sugar in a fine sieve, allow to drain thoroughly, then transfer into the hot oil and fry for 2 minutes.

5 Once the nuts have reached a deep golden brown colour, remove from the oil with a slotted spoon and transfer directly to a tray lined with baking paper. Sprinkle the hot nuts generously with sea salt.

6 Once the nuts have completely cooled they can be stored in an airtight container.

ASSEMBLING

1 Using a large serrated knife, cut the kouign-amann rings in half (as if you were cutting a bagel in half, ready to fill it). Lift the top half of each kouign-amann and place it next to its respective base.

2 Place a disc of parfait on the base of each kouign-amann, ensuring that the centre hole lines up, then place the top half of the kouign-amann on top.

3 Transfer the 300 g of double (heavy) cream into a piping bag. Cut a hole about 5 mm (¼ in) in the tip of the piping bag, and pipe 4 buttons of cream at the compass points for each of the kouign-amann.

4 Now cut a 5 mm (¼ in) hole in the tip of the chocolate ganache piping bag and, directly to the right of each button of cream, pipe a similar-sized button of ganache. Repeat with the dulce de leche. At this stage you should have an unbroken circle of alternating piped buttons of cream, ganache and dulce de leche.

5 Finally, place a candied hazelnut half, cut side up, resting on the peak of every second button, 6 hazelnut halves for each complete Paris-Brest.

Serve, to six incredibly impressed dinner party guests!

Strawberry Cheesecake Mille-Feuille

YIELDS 6

caramelised pastry

cheesecake

250 g (8¾ oz) strawberries

strawberry glaze

Around the time the Strawberry Cheesecake Mille-Feuille was featured on the Lune Lab, a friend invited me to a barbecue and asked me to bring dessert. While it may not seem so, this was quite the loaded request, as the friend in question actively dislikes sweets.

With a level of trepidation, I arrived with several servings of the mille-feuille, and much to my surprise and delight, when dessert was eventually dished up, my friend went back for seconds!

The beauty of this dish is that, while still being rich and complex, both the cheesecake and jelly are not overly sweet. With the addition of fresh strawberry, the mille-feuille makes for a perfectly elegant end to a meal.

The recipe for crème diplomat includes gelatine, as we want the diplomat to hold its shape and not ooze out of the sides of the mille-feuille.

CARAMELISED PASTRY

1 batch of pastry, rolled out to 22 × 40 cm (8½ × 16 in)

caster (superfine) sugar, for sprinkling

1   Line a large baking tray with baking paper and sprinkle an even layer of caster (superfine) sugar on the baking paper. Carefully transfer the batch of croissant pastry onto the tray by rolling the sheet of pastry onto your rolling pin, then unravelling it on top of the sugar-dusted baking paper.

2   Sprinkle the top side of the pastry with more sugar, then prove the sheet of pastry in a turned-off oven with a dish of hot water in the bottom for 3 hours. After 3 hours the pastry will appear puffy and shiny, and the sugar will have dissolved.

3   Remove the pastry from the oven, as well as the dish of hot water, and preheat the oven to 180°C fan (350°F). Place a sheet of baking paper on top of the proven pastry, then a heavy (or weighted) tray on top of the baking paper, to flatten the proven pastry.

4   Place in the oven and bake for 10 minutes.

5   After 10 minutes, take the trays with the pastry out of the oven, carefully remove the top tray and baking paper, then return to the oven for a further 5 minutes to allow the pastry to take on a deep golden colour.

6   Remove from the oven and flip the baked sheet of pastry onto a wire cooling rack, to deflate slightly. Allow to cool completely before portioning the pastry into 18 rectangles, each measuring 4 × 9 cm (1½ × 3½ in). →

CHEF NOTE   If you are serving this to dinner guests, I would recommend assembling each mille-feuille on individual plates, to minimise the amount of handling once they are fully assembled.

CHEESECAKE

375 g (13 oz) thickened cream

600 g (1 lb 5 oz) bloomy white rind sheep's milk cheese (or use cream cheese – it will give the finished dish a different and sweeter flavour, but will still work with the quantities here)

1 vanilla pod, seeds scraped

3 egg yolks

120 g (4¼ oz) caster (superfine) sugar

50 g (1¾ oz) Champagne

5 gelatine leaves (gold strength), soaked in cold water

PREPARE A DAY IN ADVANCE

1   Grease and line a deep-sided tray (about 30 × 20 cm/12 × 8 in) with baking paper.

2   Whip the thickened cream to soft peaks and reserve in the fridge.

3   In a stand mixer fitted with the flat beater, beat the cheese and vanilla seeds until smooth. Transfer the beaten cheese mixture into a different bowl and clean the bowl of the stand mixer.

4   Place the egg yolks and 20 g (¾ oz) of the caster sugar in the bowl of the stand mixer and, using the whisk attachment, whip until pale and fluffy.

5   Meanwhile, bring the remaining 100 g (3½ oz) of sugar and the Champagne to the boil in a small saucepan over a medium heat. Monitor the temperature using a sugar thermometer and take off the heat when the Champagne syrup reaches 110°C fan (230°F).

6   Add the soaked gelatine leaf to the hot syrup, whisk to dissolve, then slowly and carefully pour the sugar syrup into the egg yolks while they are still whisking. Once all the syrup is added, continue to whisk until the bowl cools down to skin temperature.

7   Fold the egg mixture through the beaten cream cheese, then finally fold through the whipped thickened cream. Pour the cheesecake mixture into the prepared tray, cover and allow to set in the fridge overnight.

STRAWBERRY GLAZE

1 kg (2 lb 4 oz) strawberries, washed, hulled and quartered

100 g (3½ oz) caster (superfine) sugar

PREPARE A DAY IN ADVANCE

1   Place the strawberries and sugar in a heatproof bowl and toss the strawberries to coat them in the sugar. Cover the bowl tightly with cling film.

2   Meanwhile, bring a pan filled one-third with water to the boil, then reduce the heat to keep the water at a simmer. Place the bowl of strawberries and sugar over the pan of simmering water and cook for 2–3 hours, until the strawberries are mushy, discoloured, and liquid has begun to leach out.

3   Remove the bowl from the pan carefully (both will be very hot) and allow to cool. Once cooled, transfer the entire contents of the bowl to a fine sieve or muslin (cheesecloth) set over a bowl or jug overnight, straining the strawberry juice from the pulp.

4   Set aside 100 g (3½ oz) of strawberry juice to serve. The remaining juice will be used to make the strawberry jelly.

STRAWBERRY JELLY

remaining strawberry juice from making the glaze

2 gelatine leaves (gold strength) per 150 g (5 oz) of strawberry juice

1   Weigh the remaining strawberry juice. For every 150 g (5 oz) of juice, soak 2 gelatine leaves in cold water for 5 minutes (for example, if you have 600 g/1 lb 5 oz of juice, soak 8 gelatine leaves).

2   In a small saucepan, heat a small amount of the strawberry juice (100 g/3½ oz) will be enough. Once boiling, add the soaked gelatine leaves and whisk until they have fully dissolved. Pour the warm strawberry and gelatine back into the rest of the cold strawberry juice and whisk lightly to combine.

3   Place a large measuring jug on a set of kitchen scales, 'tare' the scales, then pour 550 g (1 lb 3 oz) of the strawberry liquid into the jug. Now pour this measured strawberry liquid over the set cheesecake. Transfer carefully into the fridge and chill until the jelly is fully set.

CRÈME DIPLOMAT

250 g (9 oz) thickened cream, plus 50 g (1¾ oz) extra

370 g (13 oz) Vanilla Crème Pâtissière (Essentials, see page 263)

3 gelatine leaves (gold strength), soaked in cold water

grated zest of 3 lemons

1   Whip the 250 g (9 oz) thickened cream to soft peaks, reserve in the fridge until required.

2   Loosen the crème pâtissière in the bowl of a stand mixer fitted with the whisk attachment.

3   Meanwhile, heat the 50 g (1¾ oz) of cream in a small saucepan, removing it before the cream comes to the boil, add the soaked gelatine leaves and stir until the gelatine has fully dissolved.

4   Transfer the cream and gelatine into the bowl of the stand mixer with the crème pâtissière and whisk to combine.

5   Finally, fold the whipped cream and lemon zest through the crème pâtissière by hand.

6   Transfer the crème diplomat to a piping bag fitted with a size 7 round nozzle. Refrigerate until required for assembly.

ASSEMBLING

1   Take the 18 rectangles of pastry previously baked. Place one rectangle in the centre of each of the 6 serving plates.

2   Remove the set jelly cheesecake from the fridge and cut 6 portions, each measuring 4 × 9 cm (1½ x 3½ in).

3   Transfer a slice of portioned cheesecake onto each of the 6 of the rectangles of pastry, being careful to align the edges, such that the cheesecake sits flush on the pastry base.

4   Place another pastry rectangle on top of each piece of jelly cheesecake.

5   Take the piping bag of crème diplomat from the fridge and pipe 24 kisses of the crème on top of the second piece of pastry, in a three-by-eight configuration. Carefully place the third and final rectangle of pastry on top of the piped crème diplomat kisses.

6   Slice strawberries very thinly, then arrange 18 slices on top of each mille-feuille, in 2 rows of 9, ensuring that each slice overlaps slightly, for full coverage.

7   Warm the reserved 100 g (3½ oz) of strawberry juice in a small pot then very delicately brush it over the slices of strawberries. This epic version of a mille feuille is finally ready to serve!

If you have made it to the end of this recipe and have refrained from using any colourful language, I'd like to direct you to the careers page on the Lune website, where you should immediately submit your resumé.

Tiramisu

YIELDS 6

6 dessert glasses

croissant sponge

100 g (4 oz) espresso

mascarpone cream

Dutch-processed cocoa powder, for dusting

If carrot cake is my favourite cake of all time, then tiramisu is probably my favourite dessert. If it's on a restaurant's menu I have a seriously hard time saying no to pudding. It's that perfect combination of espresso-soaked savoiardi (often laced with something deliciously boozy), the decadent mascarpone and the thick layer of bitter cocoa that blankets the entire affair.

Talk about a 'pick me up' …

At Lune we often use desserts that classically do not include croissant as inspiration. The tiramisu has seen a few forms, the earliest being a tiramisu cruffin way back in 2014. It graduated to this stunning individual-serve dessert for Lune Lab in 2019. Replacing the savoiardi, croissant slices are soaked in espresso to form the base of the tiramisu. When it debuted on the Lune Lab we had several guests announce that it was the best tiramisu they'd ever had the pleasure of devouring. High praise indeed.

This recipe is a great way to use up leftover croissants, or just a great excuse to attempt making Lune croissants, so you can really take your tiramisu game to the next level.

CROISSANT SPONGE

3 croissants

100 g (3½ oz) thickened cream

100 g (3½ oz) caster (superfine) sugar

1   Preheat your oven to 160°C fan (320°F).

2   Cut the croissants into 1 cm- (½ in-) thick slices and place on a baking tray lined with baking paper.

3   Place the cream and sugar in a small saucepan over a low heat and whisk to dissolve the sugar. Once the sugar is dissolved, remove from the heat immediately – you do not want it to come to the boil.

4   Using a pastry brush, lightly coat each croissant slice with the warmed cream and sugar, then place the tray of slices in the oven and bake for 7–8 minutes: you are looking for it to be lightly golden, not hard and dry.

5   Remove from the oven and set aside to cool. →

MASCARPONE CREAM

3 egg yolks

240 g (8½ oz) caster (superfine) sugar

2 egg whites

50 g (1¾ oz) water

750 g (1 lb 10 oz) mascarpone

40 g (1½ oz) marsala

25 g (1 oz) strega

25 g (1 oz) sambucca

1   Prepare a sabayon with the egg yolks and 80 g (2¾ oz) of the sugar: place the yolks and sugar in a small heatproof bowl and set the bowl over a pan of just-simmering water. Whisk the yolks and sugar constantly, until they are light and foamy.

2   In the bowl of a stand mixer fitted with the whisk attachment, whip the egg whites to soft peaks.

3   Meanwhile, bring the remaining sugar and the water to the boil in a small saucepan over a medium heat, stirring to dissolve the sugar and create a syrup. Using a sugar thermometer, take the syrup to about 115°C fan (240°F). Once the syrup has reached this temperature, remove it from the heat and, in a slow and steady stream, carefully pour the sugar syrup into the whites while they are still whisking on low speed. Once all the sugar has been added, increase the speed of the mixer and whip until the bowl has cooled down to body temperature.

4   Carefully transfer the meringue mixture into a clean bowl, then transfer the mascarpone into the bowl of a stand mixer. With the whisk attachment, whip the mascarpone then add the 3 different alcohols. Whisk to combine. Finally, fold in the sabayon and meringue gently by hand, to create a light mascarpone cream.

5   Carefully transfer the mascarpone cream into a piping bag fitted with a size 10 round nozzle.

ASSEMBLING

1   Dip the croissant 'sponge' slices in the espresso for about 30 seconds, then flip and allow the other side to soak for 30 seconds. Repeat for all slices.

2   Place one soaked croissant 'sponge' slice in the base of each glass, taking care to keep the sides of the glass clean. Pipe a generous wiggle of mascarpone cream on the top of the croissant slice in each glass, then distribute the remaining croissant sponge slices evenly among the 6 glasses, arranging them carefully over the first layer of mascarpone cream. Pipe a final generous layer of mascarpone cream, making sure the wiggle of cream reaches the edges of the glass.

3   Finally, just before serving, using a small dust the cocoa powder generous on top of the mascarpone cream.

Toffee Apple and Whiskey Danish

YIELDS 6

6 danishes, blind baked
(see page 93)

toffee apple glaze

apple jam

whiskey crème diplomat

brown butter crumble

In the depth of winter, when daylight is fleeting, venturing outside means layering up, and summer bodies are far from our minds, nothing says 'warm bear hug' like toffee apples, whiskey, a bowl of custard and buttery pastry.

So, we decided to bring them all together in one absolute rockstar of a danish that will make dinner look like the support act... (or just skip dinner altogether and go straight to dessert).

As per the danish recipes in the Morning Tea chapter, this one is blind baked, so follow the same proving and baking instructions on page 83. The recipe calls for jazz apples, but you could also use Granny Smiths, if you would prefer the jam to be a little more tart. Feuilletine is available from specialty ingredient stores.

This recipe makes more apple jam than you will require for the six danishes, but it's a rather excellent condiment for roast pork, so, you're welcome.

APPLE JAM

500 g (1 lb 2 oz) caster (superfine) sugar

10 g (⅓ oz) jaune/yellow pectin

125 g (4½ oz) apple juice

500 g (1 lb 2 oz) jazz apples, peeled, cored and cut into quarters

10 g (⅓ oz) citric acid

PREPARE A DAY IN ADVANCE

1   Take a clean, dry medium saucepan and put it over a medium heat. Once the pan is hot, gradually sprinkle in some of the caster (superfine) sugar, wait for it to fully caramelise, then sprinkle in a little more, waiting each time until all the sugar is melted before adding more. Reserve 100 g (3½ oz) of the sugar and mix it with the pectin.

2   Once the sugar is melted and evenly caramelised, slowly add the apple juice, whisking vigorously to avoid the caramel seizing. Once all the apple juice has been incorporated, add the apples and cook for 30 minutes until they are fully transparent. Add the pectin and sugar mix, stirring constantly. Monitor the temperature of the jam with a sugar thermometer: once it reaches 106°C (223°F) add the citric acid. Remove from the heat and transfer to a large shallow tray to cool to room temperature and set.

3   Once cooled, blitz the jam briefly in a food processor in small batches; you want to keep some chunks of apple for texture throughout the jam.

4   Transfer about 200 g (7 oz) of the jam into a piping bag, and the rest into sterilised jars. →

WHISKEY CRÈME DIPLOMAT

200 g (7 oz) milk

50 g (1¾ oz) caster (superfine) sugar

4 egg yolks

10 g (⅓ oz) plain (all-purpose) flour, sifted

10 g (⅓ oz) cornflour (cornstarch), sifted

60 g (2 oz) whiskey

250 g (9 oz) double (heavy) cream

PREPARE A DAY IN ADVANCE

1 Heat the milk in a saucepan to just below boiling point, taking care to not allow a skin to form.

2 Meanwhile, whisk the caster sugar with the egg yolks in a bowl until the mixture is pale and light. Whisk in the plain (all-purpose) flour and cornflour (cornstarch) and whisk well to combine.

3 When the milk is just about to boil, pour the milk gradually into the egg mixture, whisking constantly to incorporate. Now pour the egg and milk mixture back into the pan. Whisk the mixture continually over a medium heat until it begins to boil, and carry on whisking for about 3 minutes on the boil, until the crème pâtissière reaches a nice thick consistency. Finally, add the whiskey and whisk to combine.

4 Take off the heat and pour into a clean bowl. Place cling film over the surface of the crème pâtissière to prevent a skin from forming, then store in the fridge until ready to use.

5 The following day, whisk the double (heavy) cream in the bowl of a stand mixer fitted with a whisk attachment until it forms stiff peaks.

6 Remove the set whiskey crème pâtissière from the fridge and loosen it with a large balloon whisk. Fold the whipped double cream through the whiskey crème pâtissière until it is completely homogenous and you cannot see any streaks of double cream.

7 Transfer into a piping bag fitted with a size 10 round nozzle, and reserve in the fridge until required.

CRUMBLE

250 g (9 oz) plain (all-purpose) flour

180 g (6⅓ oz) butter, cold, cut into cubes

50 g (1¾ oz) caster (superfine) sugar

70 g (2½ oz) brown sugar

5 g (0.2 oz) sea salt flakes

1 Preheat the oven to 160°C fan (320°F). Line a baking tray with baking paper.

2 Place the flour and butter into the bowl of a stand mixer fitted with the flat beater and mix on low speed until the mixture resembles coarse breadcrumbs. Add the sugars and salt and mix on low speed until the ingredients just come together to form an even crumb, with pieces about 3–5 mm (¼ in).

3 Evenly distribute the crumble on the lined baking tray and bake for 10–12 minutes until golden brown.

4 Remove from oven and allow to cool completely to room temperature.

BROWN BUTTER CRUMBLE

80 g (2¾ oz) butter

250 g (9 oz) crumble

125 g (4½ oz) feuilletine flakes

pinch of sea salt

1 Melt the butter in a small saucepan over a medium heat to beurre noisette (a process that evaporates the water out of the butter and separates the milk solids from the fat, and makes the butter take on a really nutty, toasty aroma). As soon as the butter is at beurre noisette stage, remove from the heat.

2 Place a small heatproof bowl on a set of kitchen scales, 'tare' the scales and carefully pour 60 g (2 oz) of the brown butter into the bowl, separating the from the burnt milk solids at the bottom of the pan.

3 Place the 250 g (9 oz) of crumble and 125 g (4½ oz) of feuilletine in a bowl, stir lightly to mix the two, then pour the brown butter over the dry ingredients and season with the salt, stirring to coat the crumble mix with the brown butter. Set aside until required.

TOFFEE APPLE GLAZE

100 g (3½ oz) caster (superfine) sugar

100 g (3½ oz) apple juice

3 g (0.1 oz) pectin NH

4 g (0.14 oz) citric acid

1   Once again, this recipe begins by creating a dry caramel. Take a clean, dry medium saucepan and put it over a medium heat. Once the pan is hot, gradually sprinkle in some of the sugar, wait for it to full caramelise, then sprinkle in a little more, waiting each time until all the sugar is melted before adding more. Reserve 20 g (¾ oz) of caster sugar and mix it with the pectin.

2   Once the sugar is melted and evenly caramelised, slowly add the apple juice, whisking vigorously to avoid the caramel seizing. Once all the apple juice has been incorporated, add the pectin mixture and return to the boil. Finally, add the citric acid then take off the heat and stir to combine.

FINISHING

1   Take your 6 cooled, unfilled blind-baked danish shells. Using a soft-bristled pastry brush, generously glaze the baked surfaces of the danishes with the warmed toffee apple glaze.

2   Cut a small hole, about 3 mm, in the tip of the toffee apple jam piping bag and pipe a thin layer of jam in the base of each danish (around 30 g/1 oz). If your jam is not in a piping bag, you can also just spoon the jam into the base and carefully spread the jam to fill right to the corners of the danish.

3   Now, taking your piping bag of whiskey crème diplomat, pipe a thick layer into the danish, such that the crème diplomat finishes just under the lip of the danish cavity.

4   Finally, generously cover the crème diplomat with the brown butter crumble.

Serve immediately. With a nip of whiskey.

Twice-Baked Croissants

Almond croissants came into being as an austerity measure for French bakers. If there were any croissants left over at the end of the day, they would be reserved, and the following day, transformed into croissants aux amandes; a day-old traditional croissant, soaked in sugar syrup, filled with an almond frangipane, topped with almonds, then baked again.

At Lune, the concept of the almond croissant has inspired literally hundreds of different twice-baked croissants (a term, and a revolution, which I believe started with Lune). Before Lune, I had never experienced or witnessed a twice-baked croissant that wasn't an almond croissant. The idea came to me one day, just after Cam had joined Lune and we were transitioning the little business from a wholesale bakery to a hole-in-the-wall customer-facing shop. I posed the question to Cam, 'Why is it that day-old croissants are only ever filled with almond frangipane?' Given the myriad of different nut meals, to me it seemed obvious that there was an opportunity to create an entirely new range of flavours, all from a humble day-old plain croissant. And for a business essentially founded on one pastry, it had the added bonus of drastically increasing the product line-up.

And so, the notion of the 'twice-baked croissant' evolved.

Almond Croissant

6 day-old croissants

sugar syrup

Almond Frangipane
(Essentials, see page 262)

flaked almonds

icing (powdered) sugar

At Lune, like everything else we do, almond croissants are not exactly made the traditional way. Classically, an almond croissant will be flat, and I hate to say it, often rather sad looking. The old-school way to make almond croissants is to bake them between two trays, such that they are squashed during their second bake.

This seemed like madness to me – why would you want to lose the definition of all those beautiful layers, and in the process, the crunch and flake of that buttery pastry. So, I developed a recipe and technique for the almond croissant that maintained the integrity of the structure of the croissant, while still incorporating the moist, delicious, cake-like frangipane through the centre.

The signature of a Lune almond croissant? The beautiful spine of flaked almonds that stand proud and perfect atop the croissant.

SUGAR SYRUP

500 g (17 oz) water

220 g (7¾ oz) caster (superfine) sugar

2 tablespoons kirsch

1   Place the water and sugar in a small saucepan and stir over a medium heat until all the sugar is dissolved, then bring the syrup to the boil. Once boiling, remove from the heat and add the kirsch.

ASSEMBLING AND BAKING

1   Preheat your oven to 180°C fan (350°F) and line a large baking tray with baking paper.

2   Using a large serrated knife (a bread knife will work best), cut the croissants in half. Brush the cut side of both halves of each croissant generously with the sugar syrup. Pipe a healthy wiggle of frangipane on the bottom half of each croissant then replace the top halves, cupping your hand and gently securing each top. Finish off each croissant by piping a seam of frangipane across the top, then garnish with flaked almonds, pinching as many almonds as you can together and pressing them into the frangipane, along the entire length of the seam. (How we get the flaked almonds to stand up so perfectly is one of the most frequently-asked questions at Lune. There is no magic answer. It is labour intensive, time consuming and difficult. Our chefs prepare literally hundreds of almond croissants at Lune every day, such is their popularity, hence practice makes perfect!)

3   Place the prepared croissants on the lined baking tray and bake for 18–20 minutes, until the frangipane inside is set. Check this by carefully lifting the lid of one of the croissants with a fork and checking the doneness of the frangipane. If it still looks like cake batter, it is not yet ready. Bake for a few more minutes and check again.

4   Remove from the oven and allow to cool to room temperature.

5   Once cooled, dust the almond croissants with icing (powdered) sugar and serve.

Coconut Pandan Twice Baked

YIELDS 6

6 day-old croissants

pandan sugar syrup

Coconut Frangipane
(Essentials, see page 262)

flaked coconut, to garnish

icing (powdered) sugar,
for dusting

Before joining me at Lune, Cam owned a bar in Sydney. When we started playing around with the idea of using different nut meals and flavours to create variations of the almond croissant, Cam recalled to me one of his favourite Sydney treats at a Malaysian restaurant called Mamak. He talked about rich, buttery roti, served with kaya, a spread made from pandan and coconut. Not dissimilar to the flavour profile of roti, Cam suggested that perhaps coconut and pandan were flavours that would also complement croissant pastry. And so the Coconut Pandan Twice Baked was born!

Pandan leaves can be found in most Asian grocery stores. One bunch will be sufficient for this recipe.

PANDAN WATER

1 litre (34 fl oz) water

50 g (1¾ oz) fresh pandan leaves, cleaned and dried thoroughly

PREPARE A DAY IN ADVANCE

1 Bring the water to the boil in a large saucepan then add the pandan leaves. Turn off the heat, cover the saucepan, and leave to infuse overnight. The next morning, wring out the pandan leaves well to extract all the flavour. Discard the pandan leaves.

PANDAN GANACHE

100 g (3½ oz) fresh pandan leaves, cleaned and dried thoroughly

330 g (11½ oz) coconut cream (preferably Kara)

375 g (13 oz) white chocolate

55 g (2 oz) cold butter, diced

PREPARE A DAY IN ADVANCE

1 Cut the pandan leaves into small pieces. Blend with the coconut cream until well combined and the mixture has turned green (but not brown!). Pour into a saucepan and heat until simmering. Take off the heat then cover with glad wrap and leave to steep for 10 minutes.

2 Meanwhile, weigh out the white chocolate and butter into a heatproof bowl.

3 Pass the pandan coconut cream through a sieve, reserving at least 260 g (9¼ oz) of the cream. Transfer 260 g (9¼ oz) of the heated coconut cream into a clean saucepan and once again bring to a simmer, then pour it over the white chocolate and butter, whisking to combine, ensuring that the chocolate and butter are fully melted and incorporated. The mixture should be completely smooth in texture with a light green colour. Once the ganache has cooled to room temperature, cover the bowl with cling film and leave to set overnight.

4 On the day you plan to make the coconut pandan twice bakeds, transfer the set ganache into a piping bag.

PANDAN SUGAR SYRUP

500 g (17 oz) pandan water

220 g (7¾ oz) caster (superfine) sugar

1 Place the pandan water and sugar in a small saucepan and stir over a medium heat until all the sugar is dissolved, then allow the syrup to come to the boil. Once boiling, remove from the heat. →

ASSEMBLING AND BAKING

1 Preheat your oven to 180°C fan (350°F) and line a large baking tray with baking paper.

2 Using a large serrated knife, cut the croissants in half. Brush the cut side of both halves of each croissant generously with the warm pandan sugar syrup. Pipe a healthy wiggle of coconut frangipane on the bottom half of each croissant.

3 Cut a small hole in the tip of the pandan ganache piping bag (3–4 mm), then pipe a squiggle of ganache on top of the frangipane. Repeat for each of the 6 croissant bases.

4 Replace the top half of each croissant, cupping your hand and gently securing each top. Finish each croissant off by piping a seam of coconut frangipane across the top, then garnish with flaked coconut, in a similar fashion to the almond croissant on page 207 (although I have always enjoyed the slightly more random nature of the shape of coconut flakes).

5 Place the prepared croissants on the lined baking tray and bake for 20–25 minutes, until the frangipane inside is set. Check this by carefully lifting the lid of one of the croissants with a fork and checking the doneness of the frangipane. If it still looks like cake batter, it is not yet ready. Bake for a few more minutes and check again. Make sure in the final few minutes you keep an eye on them as you don't want the coconut flakes to burn!

6 Remove from the oven and allow to cool to room temperature.

7 Once cooled, dust with icing (powdered) sugar and serve.

If any of the lucky recipients are children, you're likely to get at least one excitable comment about the croissants looking like stegosauruses!

Carrot Cake Twice Baked

6 day-old croissants

spiced brown sugar syrup

carrot and walnut frangipane

carrot cake crumble

icing (powdered) sugar,
for dusting

cream cheese icing

Carrot cake is my favourite cake on the planet.

That is all.

No, jokes. I do have more to say about carrot cake. Not all carrot cakes were created equal. I'm pretty opinionated on my 'dos and don'ts' with carrot cake.

Do include walnuts (although they must be chopped, cutting a slice of carrot cake with whole walnuts in it is destined for failure). Pecans work too, but I'm a walnut girl at heart.

Do NOT include raisins (or dried fruit of any form, for that matter). It's ALL about the cream cheese icing. I've met one person in my life that prefers carrot cake without cream cheese icing. We're not friends anymore.

DEHYDRATING THE CARROTS

500 g (1 lb 2 oz) carrots

1 The frangipane calls for 60 g (2 oz) of dried carrot and 25 g (1 oz) of the crumble. In order to end up with 85 g (3 oz) of dehydrated carrot, you will need to start with about 500 g (1 lb 2 oz) of raw carrot.

2 Preheat your oven to 70°C fan (160°F) (or as low as it will go) and line a baking tray with baking paper. You can also use a dehydrator if you have one.

3 Top and tail the carrots, peel, then grate finely. Evenly and thinly spread out the grated carrot, such that there is good airflow around the grated carrot. Place the tray of grated carrot in the oven for several hours, until it is dry, but hasn't coloured; you're simply wanting to draw the moisture out, not cook it.

CARROT PUREE

100 g (3½ oz) carrot pieces, peeled and roughly chopped

1 Cook the chopped carrot in a small saucepan of boiling water until it is soft (you should easily be able to stick a fork in it). Once the carrot is soft, drain it well, then blend until smooth.

2 Allow to cool to room temperature, then use immediately or store in an airtight container in the fridge until required. →

CARROT AND WALNUT FRANGIPANE

200 g (7 oz) butter, at room temperature

100 g (3½ oz) caster (superfine) sugar

100 g (3½ oz) brown sugar

2 eggs

100 g (3½ oz) natural almond meal

100 g (3½ oz) walnut meal

¼ teaspoon ground cinnamon

¼ teaspoon mixed spice

80 g (2¾ oz) carrot puree

60 g (2 oz) dried grated carrot

1   Beat the butter and sugar in a stand mixer fitted with a flat beater until pale and fluffy. Add the eggs one at a time, continuing to beat and waiting until each one is incorporated fully before adding the next. Scrape down the bowl after the incorporation of the first egg. Add the natural almond meal, walnut meal and the spices and combine with the mixer on low speed. Finally, add the carrot puree and dried grated carrot, and with the mixer still on low speed, combine all the ingredients.

2   Scrape the bowl down well and give it a final mix by hand to ensure all the ingredients are well incorporated. Transfer the frangipane into a piping bag fitted with a size 11 star nozzle.

CARROT CAKE CRUMBLE

100 g (3½ oz) brown sugar

¼ teaspoon ground cinnamon

¼ teaspoon mixed spice

60 g (2 oz) plain (all-purpose) flour

40 g (1½ oz) natural almond meal

40 g (1½ oz) walnut meal

25 g (1 oz) dried grated carrot

80 g (2¾ oz) butter, softened

1   Add all the dry ingredients to the bowl of a stand mixer fitted with a flat beater. Before attaching the bowl to the mixer, using a hand whisk combine the dry ingredients so they are well incorporated. Now add the softened butter, then mix on low speed until the ingredients start to bind together, forming a chunky crumble consistency. You're looking for small pebble-sized pieces of crumble.

SPICED BROWN SUGAR SYRUP

500 g (17 oz) water

150 g (5 oz) caster (superfine) sugar

100 g (3½ oz) brown sugar

1 teaspoon vanilla extract

1 cinnamon stick

pinch of mixed spice

pinch of nutmeg

1   Place all of the ingredients in a small saucepan and stir over a medium heat until the sugar has dissolved and the cinnamon has infused the syrup, then bring the syrup to the boil. Once boiling, remove from the heat.

CREAM CHEESE ICING

250 g (9 oz) cream cheese

25 g (1 oz) butter, softened

25 g (1 oz) icing (powdered) sugar, sifted

1 teaspoon lemon juice

1   Place the cream cheese in the bowl of a stand mixer fitted with the flat beater and soften the cream cheese by beating on medium-high speed for a minute or so. Add the butter and beat until smooth and homogenous. Finally add the icing (powdered) sugar and lemon juice and beat until everything is fully incorporated. Transfer to a piping bag fitted with a size 11 star nozzle.

2   If you have prepared this in advance, let it sit at room temperature for an hour or two before using.

ASSEMBLING, BAKING AND FINISHING

1   Preheat your oven to 180°C fan (350°F) and line a large baking tray with baking paper.

2   Using a large serrated knife, cut the croissants in half. Brush the cut side of both halves of each croissant generously with the spiced brown sugar syrup. Pipe a generous wiggle of carrot and walnut frangipane on the bottom half of each croissant.

3   Replace the top half of each croissant, cupping your hand and gently securing each top. Finish off each croissant by piping a seam of carrot and walnut frangipane across the top, then press chunks of carrot cake crumble into the seam of frangipane, all the way along the top of the croissant.

4   Place the prepared croissants on the lined baking tray and bake for 20–25 minutes, until the frangipane inside is set. Towards the end of the baking time, check to see if the frangipane is baked by carefully lifting the lid of the croissant. If the frangipane still looks like cake batter, it is not yet ready. Bake for a few more minutes and check again.

5   Remove from the oven and allow to cool to room temperature.

6   Once cooled completely, dust with icing sugar.

7   Finally, pipe 5 rosettes of cream cheese icing along the top of each croissant. It is important that this is done when the croissant is completely cool, otherwise the icing will melt.

CHEF NOTE   Who ever thought that carrot cake would pair so shockingly well with croissant? Your first bite will confirm that in fact it really does. Your second bite might even convince you that from this moment on, carrot cake must always be eaten with croissant. I mean, if you're skating on thin ice, you may as well tap dance …

Pecan Pie Twice Baked

YIELDS 6

6 day-old croissants

bourbon maple sugar syrup

180 g (6⅓ oz) pecan halves

icing (powdered) sugar,
for dusting

bourbon maple cream

In my humble opinion, this is far and away our best twice-baked offering. It has been on the menu for almost as long as Lune twice bakeds have existed, debuting back in August 2014, and makes a reappearance at least once a year, due to popular demand.

The clincher? The huge dollop of boozy bourbon cream we serve on top of it.

PECAN FRANGIPANE

200 g (7 oz) butter,
at room temperature

100 g (3½ oz) caster
(superfine) sugar

80 g (2¾ oz) brown sugar

1 tablespoon maple syrup
(20 g/ ¾ oz)

2 eggs

100 g (3½ oz) natural
almond meal

100 g (3½ oz) ground
roasted pecan

1 tablespoon bourbon

1   Beat the butter, sugars and maple syrup in a stand mixer fitted with a flat beater until light and fluffy. Add the eggs one at a time, continuing to beat and waiting until each one is incorporated fully before adding the next. Mix in the almond meal, ground roasted pecan and finally, the bourbon. Transfer the frangipane into a piping bag fitted with a size 11 star nozzle.

BOURBON MAPLE SUGAR SYRUP

475 g (16 oz) water

160 g (5½ oz) caster
(superfine) sugar

2 tablespoons bourbon

80 g (2¾ oz) maple syrup

1   Place the water and sugar in a small saucepan and stir over a medium heat until all the sugar has dissolved, then allow the syrup to come to the boil. Once boiling, remove from the heat and add the bourbon and maple syrup.

BOURBON MAPLE CREAM

300 g (10½ oz) thickened cream

30 g (1 oz) maple syrup

1 teaspoon bourbon

1   In a stand mixer fitted with a whisk attachment, whip the cream, maple syrup and bourbon to stiff peaks. Reserve in the fridge until ready to serve. →

ASSEMBLING AND BAKING

1 Preheat your oven to 180°C fan (350°F) and line a large baking tray with baking paper.

2 Using a large serrated knife, cut the croissants in half. Brush the cut side of both halves of each croissant generously with the warm bourbon maple sugar syrup. Pipe a generous wiggle of pecan frangipane on the bottom half of each croissant.

3 Replace the top half of each croissant, cupping your hand and gently securing each top. Finish each croissant off by piping a seam of pecan frangipane across the top, then press a handful of pecan halves into the seam of frangipane.

4 Place the prepared croissants on the lined baking tray and bake for 20–25 minutes, until the frangipane inside is set. Check this by carefully lifting the lid of one of the croissants with a fork and checking the doneness of the frangipane. If it still looks like cake batter, it is not yet ready. Bake for a few more minutes and check again.

5 Remove from the oven and allow to cool to room temperature.

6 Once cooled, dust with icing sugar. Serve with a large, rustic dollop of the bourbon whipped cream.

Macca Sacca

6 day-old croissants

sugar syrup

macadamia frangipane

Salted Caramel
(Essentials, see page 264)

300 g (10½ oz) macadamias, chopped

icing (powdered) sugar, for dusting

For the uninitiated, the Macca Sacca (as it has been known at Lune since day dot), was one of the first twice bakeds we created with a different frangipane; the legendary Macadamia Salted Caramel.

Nothing about this flavour combination is ground-breaking. But sometimes they don't have to be. A few aphorisms spring to mind; 'if it ain't broke, don't fix it', and 'there's no point reinventing the wheel'.

Macadamia, paired with salted caramel, jammed into a buttery croissant is never going to upset anyone. So, we did it. Enjoy.

MACADAMIA FRANGIPANE

200 g (7 oz) butter, at room temperature

200 g (7 oz) caster (superfine) sugar

2 eggs

100 g (3½ oz) macadamia meal

100 g (3½ oz) blanched almond meal

1   Beat the butter and sugar in a stand mixer fitted with a flat beater until pale and fluffy. Add the eggs one at a time, continuing to beat and waiting until each one is incorporated fully before adding the next. Scrape down the bowl after the incorporation of the first egg. Finally, with the mixer on low speed, mix in the macadamia meal and almond meal. Once again, scrape the bowl down well, giving it a final mix by hand (with a spatula) to ensure all the ingredients are well incorporated. Transfer the frangipane into a piping bag fitted with a size 11 star nozzle.

SUGAR SYRUP

500 g (17 oz) water

220 g (7¾ oz) caster (superfine) sugar

2 tablespoons kirsch

1   Place the water and sugar in a small saucepan and stir over a medium heat until all the sugar has dissolved, then bring the syrup to the boil. Once boiling, remove from the heat and add the kirsch. →

ASSEMBLING AND BAKING

1 Preheat your oven 180°C fan (350°F) and line a large baking tray with baking paper.

2 Using a large serrated knife, cut the croissants in half. Brush the cut side of both halves of each croissant generously with the warm sugar syrup. Pipe a healthy wiggle of macadamia frangipane on the bottom half of each croissant.

3 Cut a small hole in the tip of the salted caramel piping bag (about 4 mm), then pipe a seam of salted caramel on top of the frangipane, from one end of the croissant base to the other, then sprinkle about 15 g (½ oz) of chopped macadamia over the frangipane and salted caramel. Repeat for each of the 6 croissant bases.

4 Replace the top half of each croissant, cupping your hand and gently securing each top. Finish off each croissant by piping a seam of macadamia frangipane across the top, then press a handful of chopped macadamias into the seam of frangipane, about 30 g (1 oz) of macadamias per croissant.

5 Place the prepared croissants on the lined baking tray and bake for 20–25 minutes, until the frangipane inside is set. Check this by carefully lifting the lid of one of the croissants with a fork and checking the doneness of the frangipane. If it still looks like cake batter, it is not yet ready. Bake for a few more minutes and check again.

6 Remove from the oven and allow to cool to room temperature. Once cooled, dust with icing (powdered) sugar and serve.

As one of the easiest of the Lune twice bakeds to make, and arguably one of the most delicious, I have a sneaking suspicion this page might get a little dog-eared and fingerprinted!

Finger Bun

6 day-old croissants

strawberry syrup

milk and coconut frangipane

coconut whip icing

desiccated coconut, to garnish

If you grew up in Australia or New Zealand, you're probably no stranger to the original Finger Bun.

For those of you that are less acquainted with this ANZ delicacy, let me describe it for you. A finger bun is a sweetened white bread bun, similar in size and shape to a hotdog bun. Traditionally it also included dried fruit, but the ones that featured in my childhood were (thankfully) sans fruit. The best bit, by far, was the sickly-sweet icing that came in a couple of varieties; good old fondant, or my personal favourite, the whipped coconut icing. Before eating them, you would cut them in half and slather them with butter (and if your sweet tooth was feeling particularly demanding, also a generous lick of strawberry jam).

No doubt the finger bun has a lot of sugar highs to answer for.

In recent times there has been a bit of a revival of the old finger bun, and there was no way we were missing that boat. So the Lune 'Finger Bun' twice baked was created, and I was instantly in love. Some time after this I went back to the source of the inspiration and bought a finger bun, excited for the imminent nostalgic wave I was about to ride. Oh, the disappointment.

I only eat Lune finger buns now.

JUS FRAISE

500 g (1 lb 1¾ oz) frozen strawberries

50 g (2 oz) caster (superfine sugar)

1   Place the strawberries and sugar in a heatproof bowl and toss the strawberries to coat them in the sugar. Cover the bowl tightly with cling film.

2   Meanwhile, bring a saucepan filled one-third with water to the boil, then reduce the heat to keep the water at a simmer. Place the bowl of strawberries and sugar over the pan of simmering water and cook for 2–3 hours, until the strawberries are mushy, discoloured, and liquid has begun to leach out.

3   Remove the bowl from the pot carefully (both will be very hot) and allow to cool. Once cooled, strain the strawberries, separating the fruit pulp from the liquid. Reserve the liquid (the *jus fraise*) and the strawberry pulp. Puree the strawberry pulp. Both will be required for the Strawberry Syrup.

STRAWBERRY SYRUP

120 g (4¼oz/½ cup) strawberry puree

250 g (8½ oz) jus fraise

500 g (17 oz) water

1   Place all the ingredients in a small saucepan and stir over a medium heat, allowing the syrup to come to the boil. Once boiling, remove from the heat. →

COCONUT WHIP ICING

100 g (3½ oz) milk

100 g (3½ oz) thickened cream

15 g (½ oz) caster
(superfine) sugar

100 g (3½ oz) coconut milk
powder, sifted

300 g (10½ oz) double
(heavy) cream

1   In a small saucepan, heat the milk, cream and sugar until just simmering. Add the coconut milk powder and whisk constantly until the mixture comes to the boil. Continue to cook for a couple of minutes, whisking, allowing the mixture to thicken.

2   Take off the heat and pour into a clean heatproof bowl. Place cling film over the surface of the coconut 'base' to prevent a skin from forming, then store in the fridge overnight.

3   The following day, just before you plan to serve the finger bun twice bakeds, put the bowl of your stand mixer in the fridge for a few minutes to chill it, then transfer the coconut base into the bowl of the stand mixer fitted with the whisk attachment, along with the double (heavy) cream, and whip until it forms stiff peaks. Keep a close eye while it is whipping because there is a fine line between perfectly whipped and split!

4   This recipe makes white icing for the finger buns. If you'd prefer pink icing, add a tiny drop of pink food colouring just before whipping the coconut base and double cream.

5   Transfer into a piping bag fitted with a size 11 round nozzle.

MILK AND COCONUT FRANGIPANE

200 g (7 oz) butter,
at room temperature

200 g (7 oz) caster
(superfine) sugar

pinch of salt

2 eggs

100 g (3½ oz) milk powder

75 g (2½ oz) desiccated coconut

75 g (2½ oz) blanched
almond meal

1   Beat the butter, sugar and salt in a stand mixer fitted with a flat beater until pale and fluffy. Add the eggs one at a time, continuing to beat and waiting until each one is incorporated fully before adding the next. Scrape down the bowl after the incorporation of the first egg. Finally, with the mixer on low speed, mix in the milk powder, almond meal and desiccated coconut. Once again, scrape the bowl down well, giving it a final mix by hand (with a spatula) to ensure all the ingredients are well incorporated. Transfer the frangipane into a piping bag fitted with a size 11 star nozzle.

ASSEMBLING, BAKING AND FINISHING

1 Preheat your oven to 180°C fan (350°F) and line a large baking tray with baking paper.

2 Using a large serrated knife, cut the croissants in half. Brush the cut side of both halves of each croissant generously with the warm strawberry syrup. Pipe a healthy wiggle of milk and coconut frangipane on the bottom half of each croissant.

3 Cut a small hole in the tip of the strawberry jam piping bag (3–4 mm), then pipe a squiggle of jam on top of the frangipane. Repeat for each of the 6 croissant bases.

4 Replace the top half of each croissant, cupping your hand and gently securing each top. The finger bun is a unique twice-baked at Lune, as it does not get any garnish before being baked.

5 Place the prepared croissants on the lined baking tray and bake for 20–25 minutes, until the frangipane inside is set. Check this by carefully lifting the lid of one of the croissants with a fork and checking the doneness of the frangipane. If it still looks like cake batter, it is not yet ready. Bake for a few more minutes and check again.

6 Remove from the oven and allow to cool completely to room temperature. If you try to ice the finger buns while they are still warm the icing will simply melt and slide off.

7 Once cooled, the finger buns can be iced. Holding the piping bag with coconut whip at one end of the croissant and begin piping, zigzagging left to right, making your zig-zag bigger as you approach the 'nose' of the croissant, then reducing it as you reach the other end, aiming for a diamond shape. Repeat for each of the 6 baked croissants.

8 The pièce de résistance of the finger bun is the chewy desiccated coconut that coats the coconut whip icing. Very carefully holding the pastry from beneath, dip the icing into a bowl of desiccated coconut, making sure to dip as gently as possible – you don't want to flatten your beautiful squiggle of icing. Serve immediately!

CHEF NOTE This recipe makes white icing for the finger buns. If you'd prefer pink icing, add a tiny drop of pink food colouring just before whipping the coconut base and double cream.

Mocha Twice Baked

6 day-old croissants

espresso sugar syrup

espresso hazelnut frangipane

Dark Chocolate Ganache
(Essentials, see page 264)

coffee crème pâtissière

coffee icing drizzle

icing (powdered) sugar

180 g (6⅓ oz) chopped
hazelnuts

A recipe for those of us who love our coffee, and are lucky enough to have access to espresso coffee at home! Every element of this twice baked incorporates lifegiving caffeine, so I'd recommend preparing these for a morning treat, otherwise you may be awake all night from the coffee and sugar high!

Normally I would consider this recommendation absolute sacrilege, but a friend once told me that stashing a Mocha Twice Baked in the fridge, then serving cold slices of it with vanilla ice cream, was her guilty pleasure. I can confirm she is absolutely right.

ESPRESSO HAZELNUT FRANGIPANE

200 g (7 oz) butter,
at room temperature

200 g (7 oz) caster
(superfine) sugar

2 eggs

30 g (1 oz) espresso (1 shot)

100 g (3½ oz) natural
almond meal

100 g (3½ oz) hazelnut meal

1 Beat the butter and sugar in a stand mixer fitted with a flat beater until pale and fluffy.

2 Add the eggs one at a time, continuing to beat and waiting until each one is incorporated fully before adding the next, then add the espresso and beat until incorporated.

3 Mix in the natural almond meal and hazelnut meal. Scrape the bowl down well and give it a final mix by hand to ensure all the ingredients are well incorporated.

4 Transfer the frangipane into a piping bag fitted with a size 11 star nozzle.

COFFEE CRÈME PATISSIÈRE

300 g (10½ oz) milk

½ vanilla pod, seeds scraped

30 g (1 oz) espresso (1 shot)

50 g (1¾ oz) caster
(superfine) sugar

4 egg yolks

10 g (⅓ oz) plain
(all-purpose) flour, sifted

10 g (⅓ oz) cornflour
(cornstarch), sifted

1 Heat the milk, vanilla and espresso in a saucepan to just below boiling point, taking care to not allow a skin to form.

2 Meanwhile, put the caster (superfine) sugar and egg yolks in a bowl and whisk well to combine, until the mixture is pale and light. Whisk in the plain (all-purpose) flour and cornflour (cornstarch) and whisk well again to combine.

3 When the milk is just about to boil, pour the milk gradually into the egg mixture, whisking constantly to incorporate. Now pour the egg and milk mixture back into the pan. Whisk the mixture continually over a medium heat until it begins to boil, and carry on whisking for about 3 minutes on the boil, until the crème pâtissière reaches a nice thick consistency.

4 Take off the heat and pour into a clean bowl. Place cling film over the surface of the crème pâtissière to prevent a skin from forming, then store in the fridge until ready to use.

5 Just before assembling the mocha twice bakeds, take the coffee crème pâtissière from the fridge, remove the cling film, and loosen with a whisk. Fill a piping bag with the custard and transfer the remaining into a sealed container and reserve in the fridge.

1 Transfer the room-temperature chocolate ganache into a piping bag. It is important that the ganache has been allowed to firm up a little as you want it to hold its shape when piped. →

ESPRESSO SUGAR SYRUP

500 g (17 oz) water

220 g (7¾ oz) caster (superfine) sugar

60 g (2 oz) espresso (2 shots)

1   Place the water and sugar in a small saucepan and stir over a medium heat until all the sugar has dissolved, then bring the syrup to the boil. Once boiling, remove from the heat and add the espresso.

COFFEE ICING DRIZZLE

500 g (1 lb 2 oz) icing (powdered) sugar, sifted

30 g (1 oz) espresso (1 shot)

1 teaspoon milk (optional)

Mix all the ingredients together until thick, but still runny enough to drizzle. If it is too thick, add a teaspoon of milk, whisk in the milk and check the consistency again. Once you are happy with the 'drizzle factor' of the icing, immediately transfer it into a disposable piping bag.

ASSEMBLING, BAKING AND FINISHING

1   Preheat your oven to 180°C fan (350°F) and line a large baking tray with baking paper.

2   Using a large serrated knife, cut the croissants in half. Brush the cut side of both halves of each croissant generously with the warm espresso sugar syrup. Pipe a generous wiggle of espresso hazelnut frangipane on the bottom half of each croissant.

3   Cut a small hole in the tip of the chocolate ganache piping bag (3–4 mm), then pipe a squiggle of ganache on top of the frangipane. Repeat for each of the 6 croissant bases.

4   Now cut a slightly bigger hole (5–6 mm) in the tip of the coffee crème pâtissière piping bag and pipe one long seam, end to end, along the base of each croissant, on top of the squiggle of chocolate ganache. Repeat for each of the 6 croissant bases.

5   Replace the top half of each croissant, cupping your hand and gently securing each top. Finish each croissant off by piping a seam of espresso hazelnut frangipane across the top, then press a handful of chopped hazelnuts into the frangipane seam.

6   Place the prepared croissants on the lined baking tray and bake for 20–25 minutes, until the frangipane inside is set. Unlike other twice bakeds, because the Mocha incorporates both chocolate ganache and coffee crème pat inside the croissant, checking to see if the frangipane is baked by carefully lifting the lid of the croissant will not be an accurate test, as we have introduced more moisture to the filling. If you have baked any of the previous twice baked recipes, apply the same baking time for the Mocha that was required for them.

7   Remove from the oven and allow to cool to room temperature.

8   Once cooled, dust with icing sugar. Finally, cut a tiny hole in the tip of the coffee icing drizzle piping bag and, zigzagging back and forth over the croissant, drizzle the coffee icing across the top of the Mocha Twice Baked.

Wait only as long as it takes for the coffee icing drizzle to set before serving, perhaps paired with a flat white?

Choc Chip Cookie

6 day-old pains au chocolat

'cookie' sugar syrup

cookie frangipane

raw cookie dough

200 g (7 oz) Callebaut milk chocolate chips, 90 g (3¼ oz) for filling, the rest for garnish

dulcey ganache

pre-baked cookies

sea salt flakes

At Lune we don't just *twice bake* leftover traditional croissants, the pain au chocolat also gets a dressing up!

The Choc Chip Cookie is one of the most popular pain au chocolat twice bakeds we've offered over the years.

I have to warn you, the choc chip cookies that garnish the pastry are pretty addictive all on their own, so (not that I'm an enabler) I've increased the quantities for the choc chip cookie recipe so there will safely be leftovers for snacking.

All the way back in the Afternoon Tea chapter I spoke about marie biscuits. They also get a mention in this recipe. If you don't have access to Marie biscuits, Graham Crackers or digestive biscuits are a fine substitute. You will also see 'Dulcey' chocolate referred to in this recipe. If you can't get your hands on Valrhona's Dulcey chocolate, any brand of chocolate that has a line of caramelised white chocolate will work.

SALTED CHOCOLATE CHIP COOKIES

225 g (8 oz) butter, at room temperature

175 g (6 oz) brown sugar

115 g (4 oz) caster (superfine) sugar

1 egg

1 teaspoon vanilla extract

275 g (9¾ oz) plain (all-purpose) flour

15 g (½ oz) milk powder

1 teaspoon baking powder

½ teaspoon bicarbonate of soda (baking soda)

1 teaspoon sea salt flakes

340 g (12 oz) milk chocolate chips

PREPARE A DAY IN ADVANCE

1   Cream the butter and sugars in the bowl of a stand mixer fitted with a flat beater until pale and fluffy. Add the egg and vanilla extract and beat until fully incorporated.

2   Sift all the dry ingredients into a separate bowl and, using a hand whisk, combine them such that they are evenly distributed throughout.

3   Add the dry ingredients to the creamed butter, sugar and egg and mix on low speed until the dry ingredients are fully incorporated. Finally, add the milk chocolate chips and mix on low speed until evenly distributed.

4   The cookie is used in two applications in this pastry, similar to the crumble on top of the Carrot Cake Twice Baked: little lumps of unbaked cookie dough will be pressed on top of the pain au chocolat before it is baked. Once baked, broken cookie also garnishes the finished pastry.

UNBAKED TOPPING

1   Crumble the cookie dough into little pebble-sized lumps, store in an airtight container and reserve in the fridge until required. You will require 30 g (1 oz) of cookie dough crumble for each pastry, so reserve 180 g (6⅓ oz) of the cookie dough for the unbaked topping. →

GARNISH

1 Shape the remaining dough into 50 g (1¾ oz) balls. Preheat your oven to 160°C fan (320°F) and line a couple of baking trays with baking paper. Arrange the cookie dough balls on the lined baking trays, spacing the balls about 10 cm (4 in) apart. Bake for 10 minutes, then spin your tray to allow for even heat distribution and bake for a further 3–4 minutes.

2 If you are a chewy cookie person (as I am), you will want to pull the cookies out after they have had 13 minutes of cooking time. If you prefer them on the crunchier side, leave them in for a little longer.

3 Allow to cool completely before packing away into an airtight container.

DULCEY GANACHE

175 g (6 oz) thickened cream

250 g (9 oz) Dulcey chocolate chips

18 g (½ oz) liquid glucose

350 g (12 oz) cold thickened cream (additional)

PREPARE A DAY IN ADVANCE

1 Heat the 175 g (6 oz) of thickened cream in a small saucepan to just before boiling point.

2 Weigh the Dulcey chocolate buttons and glucose into a heatproof bowl.

3 Pour the cream over the prepared ingredients in the heatproof bowl and whisk until the mixture has a smooth consistency. If the chocolate is not fully melting, put your heatproof bowl over a double boiler or bain marie (a saucepan one-third full of simmering water) and continue whisking to melt the chocolate.

4 Once the chocolate is melted and the mix is fully emulsified, remove from the double boiler and start to pour in the second addition of thickened cream, whisking to combine while you pour.

5 Cover the bowl of ganache and refrigerate overnight.

6 The following day, transfer the ganache to the bowl of a stand mixer fitted with the whisk attachment and whip gently until stiff peaks form, being careful that it doesn't split. Transfer into a piping bag.

7 Weigh the Dulcey chocolate buttons and glucose into a heatproof bowl.

8 Pour the cream over the prepared ingredients in the heatproof bowl and whisk until the mixture has a smooth consistency. If the chocolate is not fully melting, put your heatproof bowl over a double boiler or bain marie (a saucepan one-third full of simmering water) and continue whisking to melt the chocolate.

9 Once the chocolate is melted and the mix is fully emulsified, remove from the double boiler and start to pour in the second addition of thickened cream, whisking to combine while you pour.

10 Cover the bowl of ganache and refrigerate overnight.

11 The following day, transfer the ganache to the bowl of a stand mixer fitted with the whisk attachment and whip gently until stiff peaks form, being careful that it doesn't split. Transfer into a piping bag.

MARIE BISCUIT FRANGIPANE

200 g (7 oz) butter, at room temperature

120 g (4¼ oz) brown sugar

80 g (2¾ oz) caster (superfine) sugar

2 eggs

120 g (4¼ oz) marie biscuits

40 g (1½ oz) rolled oats

40 g (1½ oz) plain (all-purpose) flour

pinch of salt

1 Beat the butter and sugars in a stand mixer fitted with a flat beater until pale and fluffy.

2 Add the eggs one at a time, waiting until each one is incorporated fully before adding the next. Scrape down the bowl after the incorporation of the first egg.

3 In a food processor, blitz the marie biscuits to a fine crumb, similar to the texture of almond meal. Then also blitz the oats to a fine crumb.

4 In a bowl, combine the blitzed marie biscuit, oats and flour and mix well with a hand whisk.

5 With the mixer on low speed, add the dry ingredients and the salt. Once again, scrape the bowl down well, giving it a final mix by hand (with a spatula) to ensure all the ingredients are well incorporated.

6 Transfer the frangipane into a piping bag fitted with a size 11 star nozzle.

'COOKIE' SUGAR SYRUP

500 g (20 fl oz) water

220 g (7¾ oz) brown sugar

2 tablespoons Frangelico

1 Place the water and brown sugar in a small saucepan and stir over a medium heat until all the sugar has dissolved, then bring the syrup to the boil. Once boiling, remove from the heat and add the Frangelico.

ASSEMBLING, BAKING AND FINISHING

1 Preheat your oven to 180°C fan (350°F) and line a large baking tray with baking paper.

2 Using a large serrated knife, carefully cut the 6 pains au chocolat in half. Brush the cut side of both halves of each pain au choc generously with the warm 'cookie' sugar syrup. Pipe a healthy wiggle of cookie frangipane, completely covering the bottom half of each pastry, then sprinkle about 15 g (½ oz) of milk chocolate chips over the frangipane, followed by a pinch of sea salt flakes. Repeat for each of the 6 bases.

3 Replace the top half of each pain au chocolat, cupping your hand and gently securing each top. Finish off each pastry by piping a seam of cookie frangipane across the top, just enough to be able to press a few pieces of raw cookie dough into the frangipane seam, approximately 30 g (1 oz) per pastry.

4 Place the prepared pastries on the lined baking tray and bake for 20–25 minutes, until the frangipane inside is set.

5 Remove from the oven and allow to cool completely to room temperature.

6 Once the pains au chocolat are cool, place 110 g (3¾ oz) of milk chocolate chips into a heatproof bowl and either melt over a double boiler or in the microwave. When fully melted and still warm, transfer the melted chocolate into a small disposable piping bag.

7 Cut a 1–2 mm hole in the tip of the piping bag and, working quickly, drizzle the chocolate over the top of each pastry, working in a fast left-to-right motion.

8 Allow a few minutes for the chocolate to cool and set, then, just before you are ready to serve, cut a 4 mm (½ in) hole in the tip of the piping bag of Dulcey ganache, and pipe 5 random little kisses on top of the pastry, in amongst the clumps of baked cookie.

9 Finally, break some of the pre-baked cookies into small, odd-sized pieces, and using the kisses of ganache to help them stay in place, secure 5 little pieces of broken choc chip cookie to the top of the pastry.

If you've already eaten half of the baked cookies by the time you get to the end of this recipe, I don't blame you; they are the staff snack of choice at Lune!

Special Occasions

The first ever 'special occasion' pastry we created was an Easter egg-inspired cruffin. Needless to say, as it doesn't feature in this book you can safely assume it wasn't one of our best!

In the early days of Lune, Cam and I would change the flavours *every single week*. I now recognise this as madness, but we would spend the early part of the week brainstorming, then madly developing at least two cruffin flavours, a special twice baked, and a special savoury. This all ended infamously in tears one Saturday evening when we had a huge blow-up over a ruined batch of orange curd which had been destined for a Jaffa-inspired cruffin.

I digress. In the days leading up to Easter we master-minded this Easter egg cruffin. Roll on to Thursday night, hours before the Easter long weekend. After wrapping up the day of production around 8pm, we set about trying to procure the small chocolate easter eggs that would garnish the cruffin. Every supermarket in a 5km radius was sold out of the dastardly little chocolate beasts. Desperate, at approximately 10pm we turned our attention to petrol stations, where we finally found, what I am convinced were the last remaining easter eggs in the greater Melbourne area.

We're a bit more organised with our special occasion pastries these days, and this chapter features some of our very best.

Anzac Biscuit Kouign-Amann

YIELDS 6

6 springform tins,
11 cm (4½ in) in diameter

1 batch of pastry, rolled out
and marked for kouign-amann,
trimmed to a rectangle 40 × 20
cm (15½ x 8 in)

100 g (3½ oz) butter,
softened, for the tins

100 g (3½ oz) caster
(superfine) sugar, for the tins

100 g (3½ oz) brown sugar,
for the tins

sea salt flakes

Anzac biscuit 'batter'

In 2011, an article published in the *New York Times* quoted the kouign-amann as 'the fattiest pastry in all of Europe'.

If that is the case, then this surely must be the fattiest pastry in all the world. But we don't think about this when we sink our teeth into the decadent buttery masterpiece that beholds us. And if you've spent nearly four days labouring over your kitchen benchtop to make this, your first bite may well be the most satisfying mouthful of food you've ever had the pleasure of taking.

ANZAC BISCUIT 'BATTER'

150 g (5 oz) rolled oats

125 g (4½ oz) butter

125 g (4½ oz) caster
(superfine) sugar

125 g (4½ oz) brown sugar

125 g (4½ oz) golden syrup

150 g (5 oz) desiccated
(shredded) coconut

1   Lightly pulse the oats in a food processor.

2   Cream the butter and sugars together in the bowl of a stand mixer fitted with a flat beater until pale and fluffy. Add the golden syrup, beat on high speed to combine, then add the oats and coconut.

3   Line a baking tray with baking paper then tip the batter onto the tray, using a spatula to spread it out and flatten it into a rough rectangle. Refrigerate.

4   Once it has firmed up, carefully slide the baking paper off the tray, place another piece on top of the chilled batter and, using a rolling pin, flatten out the Anzac biscuit batter to a thickness of about 3 mm, then remove the top piece of baking paper and trim to a rectangle 36 × 18 cm (14 × 7 in).

5   Replace the top piece of baking paper and store in the fridge until required.

TIN PREPARATION

1   Place the caster (superfine) sugar and brown sugar in a bowl and whisk to combine both sugars.

2   Brush the springform tins with a liberal amount of softened butter, then tip some of the sugar mix into each tin and toss around to coat the base and sides evenly. The quantity of sugar isn't too important, as you will tip out any excess sugar that doesn't stick to the buttered tins. Keep excess sugar for shaping the kouign-amann later. Finally, sprinkle a pinch of sea salt flakes over the base of each tin. Place tins on a baking tray and set aside. →

SHAPING

1   Take the sheet of Anzac Biscuit batter out of the fridge, peel off the top layer of baking paper and, in one fast and confident motion, flip the biscuit batter onto the pastry, centred such that there is 2 cm (¾ in) of pastry left biscuit-free at the top and bottom. Press gently to stick the biscuit batter to the pastry, the carefully peel the other piece of paper off the biscuit.

2   Starting at the left-hand side, pinch and tuck the top edge of pastry over the biscuit. Now begin gently rolling the entire log of pastry and biscuit towards you, checking to make sure you are maintaining straight left and right edges. Finish the roll with the join on the underside of the log.

3   Now lay a ruler along the length of the log, and using a paring knife, make small marks at 3 cm (1¼ in) increments, measuring for 6 kouign-amann in total. Using a serrated bread knife, taking long sawing motions, slice through the log at each 3 cm (1¼ in) mark.

4   Carefully picking up one kouign-amann so as not to allow it to unravel, dip both the top and bottom surfaces in the reserved mixed sugar, then place in a prepared tin. Repeat for the remaining pastries.

5   Arrange the tins with the shaped Anzac biscuit kouign-amann on a baking tray and reserve in the fridge until you are ready to begin proving.

PROVING

1   Place your tray of Anzac biscuit KAs in a turned-off oven with a dish of boiling water in the bottom and allow to prove for 5–6 hours. They are ready when they are at least doubled in size, and touching the sides of the tin. The sugar will appear wet.

BAKING

1   Remove the tray of proven KAs from your oven, then heat it to 210°C fan (410°F). While your oven is warming up, chill the KAs in the fridge; this will help them to hold their shape during baking.

2   Once your oven is at temperature, remove the tray of KAs from the fridge and load immediately into the oven. Bake for 5 minutes at 210°C fan (410°F), then knock your oven back to 160°C fan (320°F) and bake for a further 5 minutes. During this time, prepare a second baking tray with baking paper and set it on your benchtop next to a heatproof cooling rack.

3   At this 10-minute mark, remove your KAs from the oven, set the tray down on the heatproof cooling rack and, using oven mitts, very carefully pick up each tin and flip it upside-down onto the clean baking tray, lifting the empty tin carefully off the flipped pastry so as not to damage any of the outer layers that may be inclined to stick to the tin. The pastry is underbaked at this point, and the sugar is molten, so proceed with extreme caution. Using an offset palette knife, carefully transfer each flipped kouign-amann back into the tins.

4   Place the tray of flipped KAs back into the oven at 160°C fan (320°F) for a further 10–12 minutes. They are ready when they have achieved a deep golden colour that is only ever so slightly paler in the centre.

5   Once removed from the oven, as quickly as is safe to do so, using oven mitts turn the baked pastries out of their tins and onto the clean tray, ensuring that they are not touching each other.

6   Allow to cool completely to room temperature before serving; the beauty of this pastry is not when it is still warm out of the oven.

When it has cooled, the pastry becomes one with the chewy oat and coconut batter, no beginning and no end, sweet and salty bliss. Pastry nirvana.

Birthday Cake Twice Baked

YIELDS 6

6 day-old croissants

milk syrup

'birthday cake' frangipane

crumble topping

vanilla buttercream

coloured sprinkles, to garnish

icing (powdered) sugar,
for dusting

I am often asked who my idols are. I don't really have idols. There are a few people close to me that I look up to and am constantly inspired by. But I think that's different to idolising someone. Rather, I'd call them role models.

There's one person in the cuisine world who I don't know but I certainly look up to. Christina Tosi. Her style of pastry, while very different to mine, plays on childhood reminiscence. I love how she innovates to create edible experiences that trigger delicious memories from more innocent times.

This twice baked is somewhat of an ode to Christina. Since it hit the menu back in 2017 it's made an annual appearance, funnily enough, either around the time of my birthday or Lune's birthday!

Note for this recipe: not all sprinkles were created equal. Firstly, where you live they may be known instead as 'Hundreds and Thousands', 'jimmies' or 'hagelslag' (hi there, Netherlands!). They also come in a couple of different forms; my personal favourite, the long thin miniature baton shape, which have a slightly softer musk-stick-like texture, and the tiny, much crunchier spherical variety.

'BIRTHDAY CAKE' FRANGIPANE

200 g (7 oz) butter

120 g (4¼ oz) brown sugar

2 eggs

1 teaspoon vanilla extract

70 g (2½ oz) buttermilk

120 g (4¼ oz) plain (all-purpose) flour, sifted

100 g (3½ oz) blanched almond meal

pinch of salt

1   Beat the butter and sugar in a stand mixer fitted with a flat beater until pale and fluffy.

2   Add the eggs one at a time, waiting until each one is incorporated fully before adding the next, adding the vanilla with the second egg. Scrape down the bowl after the incorporation of the first egg.

3   Mix in the buttermilk with the flour and almond meal with the mixer on low speed. Once again, scrape the bowl down well, giving it a final mix by hand (with a spatula) to ensure all the ingredients are well incorporated. The frangipane will be a little softer than normal, due to the addition of buttermilk, so cover the bowl with cling film and transfer to the fridge for an hour to firm up.

4   Just before assembly of the croissants, transfer the frangipane into a piping bag fitted with a size 11 star nozzle.

CRUMBLE TOPPING

250 g (9 oz) butter, softened

230 g (8 oz) plain (all-purpose) flour, sifted

100 g (3½ oz) custard powder, sifted

90 g (3¼ oz) icing (powdered) sugar, sifted

1 tablespoon sprinkles

1   Put the softened butter in the bowl of a stand mixer fitted with a flat beater and beat until pale and creamy.

2   Add the flour, custard powder, icing (powdered) sugar and sprinkles and mix on low speed until the ingredients start to bind together, forming a chunky crumble consistency. You're looking for small pebble-sized pieces of crumble.

3   Transfer to a container and store in the fridge until required. →

MILK SYRUP

500 g (17 oz) milk

250 g (9 oz) caster (superfine) sugar

1 tablespoon vanilla extract

1   Place all of the ingredients in a small saucepan and stir over a medium heat until the sugar has dissolved. Remove from the heat.

VANILLA BUTTERCREAM

2 egg whites, at room temperature

200 g (7 oz) caster (superfine) sugar

60 g (2 oz) water

250 g (9 oz) butter, at room temperature

1 tablespoon lemon juice

1 teaspoon vanilla extract

1   In the bowl of a stand mixer fitted with the whisk attachment, whip the egg whites to soft peaks.

2   Meanwhile, bring the sugar and water to the boil in a small saucepan, stirring to dissolve the sugar and create a syrup. Using a candy thermometer, take the syrup to between 115 and 118°C (240–244°F).

3   Once the syrup has reached this temperature, remove from the heat and, in a slow and steady stream, carefully pour the sugar syrup into the egg whites while they are still whisking on low speed.

4   Once all the sugar has been added, increase the speed of the mixer and whip until the bowl has cooled down to body temperature.

5   Cut the room-temperature butter into 2 cm (¾ in) pieces and begin gradually adding the butter to the whisking meringue, two or three pieces at a time, whisking well between each addition of butter to ensure that it is fully incorporated.

6   Once all butter is in, add the lemon juice and vanilla, and beat well to combine.

7   Transfer to a piping bag fitted with a size 11 star nozzle.

ASSEMBLING, BAKING AND FINISHING

1   Preheat your oven to 180°C fan (350°F) and line a large baking tray with baking paper.

2   Using a large serrated knife, cut the croissants in half. Brush the cut side of both halves of each croissant generously with the warm milk syrup. Pipe a generous wiggle of 'birthday cake' frangipane on the bottom half of each croissant. Before replacing the lids of the croissants, distribute a generous pinch of sprinkles over the top of the frangipane.

3   Replace the top half of each croissant, cupping your hand and gently securing each top. Finish off each croissant by piping a seam of birthday cake frangipane across the top, then press chunks of crumble topping into the seam of frangipane, all the way along the top of the croissant.

4   Place the prepared croissants on the lined baking tray and bake for 20–25 minutes, until the frangipane inside is set.

5   Remove from the oven and allow to cool completely to room temperature.

6   Once cooled, dust with icing (powdered) sugar.

7   Finally, pipe 6 or 7 kisses of vanilla buttercream randomly over top of the pastry, then garnish the buttercream kisses with yet more sprinkles. It is important that this is done when the croissant is completely cool, otherwise the buttercream will melt.

If you love croissants and you also love birthday cake, this may well be your new favourite way to celebrate that one special day of the year that is simply all about you.

CHEF NOTE This buttercream is made using the Italian meringue method.

Hot Cross Cruffin

YIELDS 6

6 proven and unbaked cruffins

flour paste for the cross

glaze

spiced fruit custard

The Hot Cross Cruffin has appeared on the Lune menu at Easter every year since its inception back in 2014. We thought the hot cross cruffin was a bit of tongue-in-cheek fun, but it really has inspired a passionate legion of fans over the years and been a surprise instant hit (and I say surprise because I really love a good old classic hot cross bun).

In 2020, for the first time in Lune's history, we had to introduce online pre-order of our pastries. This timing also coincided with Easter, traditionally a very busy time of year for Lune. The day the ordering system went live, in six short minutes, we already had orders for more than 1300 Hot Cross Cruffins alone! Which was a huge problem, because we only had enough tins to make 500 cruffins! A panicked search ensued to procure all of the cruffin tins we could get our hands on from retailers around Melbourne. It was also the first time we had a true indication of the real demand for the hot cross cruffin.

Unlike the other cruffin recipes featured in this book, this recipe starts at the point where the cruffins are proven, egg-washed and ready to be baked.

SPICED FRUIT CUSTARD

300 g (10½ oz) milk

½ vanilla pod, seeds scraped

½ teaspoon ground cinnamon

¼ teaspoon star anise

¼ teaspoon mixed spice

pinch of nutmeg

50 g (1¾ oz) caster (superfine) sugar

4 egg yolks

10 g (⅓ oz) plain (all-purpose) flour

10 g (⅓ oz) cornflour (cornstarch)

pinch of salt

35 g (1¼ oz) sultanas

30 g (1 oz) mixed peel

grated zest of 1 lemon

PREPARE A DAY IN ADVANCE

1   Put the milk, vanilla and spices in a small saucepan and heat until it's just about to reach boiling point. Reduce to barely a simmer, allowing the spices to infuse the milk while you are preparing the other ingredients.

2   Meanwhile, put the caster (superfine) sugar and egg yolks in a bowl and whisk well to combine, until the mixture is pale and light. Add the plain (all-purpose) flour and cornflour (cornstarch) and salt and again whisk well to combine.

3   Pour the warm spiced milk gradually into the egg mixture, whisking constantly to incorporate. Pour the egg and milk mixture back into the pan and whisk the mixture continually over a medium heat until it begins to boil, and carry on whisking for about 3 minutes on the boil, until the custard reaches a nice thick consistency.

4   Remove from the heat then fold through the sultanas, mixed peel and lemon zest.

5   Transfer into a clean heatproof bowl. Place cling film over the surface of the custard to prevent a skin from forming, then store in the fridge until ready to use.

6   Just before finishing the cruffins, take the custard out of the fridge, remove the cling film, and loosen the custard with a whisk, then load it into a piping bag. →

FLOUR PASTE FOR THE CROSS

160 g (5½ oz) plain (all-purpose) flour

2 g baking powder

2 g salt

2 g sugar

160 g (5½ oz) water

30 g (1 oz) oil

1   Place all the ingredients in the bowl of a stand mixer fitted with a flat beater. Mix on low-medium speed until all the ingredients are fully combined. Transfer to a piping bag.

GLAZE

120 g (4¼ oz) caster (superfine) sugar

120 g (4¼ oz) water

1   Bring the sugar and water to the boil in a small saucepan, stirring to ensure that the sugar has fully dissolved. Once at the boil, remove from the heat.

BAKING

1   Preheat your oven to 210°C fan (410°F).

2   Cut a small hole in the tip of the piping bag that holds the flour paste (about 3 mm) then, working carefully but quickly, pipe crosses over the top of the egg-washed cruffins.

3   Load into the preheated oven and bake at 210°C fan (410°F) for 5 minutes. After the first 5 minutes of baking, knock the oven back to 160°C fan (320°F) and bake for a further 15 minutes. After this phase, open the oven door and, using oven mitts, carefully spin the tray 180 degrees and bake for a final 6 minutes, until the tops of the cruffins are a deep golden brown.

4   The cruffins are fully baked when you can carefully spin one in its tin, such that the outer layers of pastry are no longer sticking to the tin.

5   Once baked, rest the cruffins for 5 minutes in their tins, then transfer from the tins to a wire cooling rack. Immediately brush the warm glaze over the top of the still-warm hot cross cruffins.

6   Cool on a wire rack for a further 20 minutes.

FINISHING

1   Create a hole in the bottom of each cruffin. This is different to the other cruffin recipes, where the hole is created in the top of the cruffin. In this instance, you don't want to damage the cross, so the filling is inserted into the bottom of the cruffin instead.

2   Pick up one cruffin, and holding it upside down (carefully such that you don't touch the glaze too much), insert a paring knife into the centre of the bottom of the cruffin, about three-quarters of the way deep, making sure not to cut all the way through to the top. This incision will allow you to poke piping bags into the cruffin to fill it.

3   Place a single cruffin on a set of digital kitchen scales and 'tare' the scales to zero, then pipe 45 g (1½ oz) of spiced fruit custard into the hole in the bottom of the cruffin, ensuring the tip of the piping bag is inserted quite far into the cruffin before piping. Turn the cruffin the right way up and return to the wire rack. Repeat this step for the rest of the cruffins.

CHEF NOTE   Before serving, I'd recommend quickly locking your front door. There may well be a large line of people waiting patiently to purchase their dozen hot cross cruffins … just saying.

Persian Love Cake

YIELDS 6

6 day-old croissants

rosewater syrup

Pistachio and Rosewater
Frangipane (Essentials,
see page 262)

Persian love cake

200 g (7 oz) pearl sugar,
for topping

200 g (7 oz) slivered green
pistachios, for topping

rosewater butter cream

dried rose petals, to garnish

Not only does this twice-baked croissant taste magnificent,
it also is visually stunning, and as such, it makes a yearly
comeback at Lune, either for Valentine's Day or Mother's Day.

That being said, it's also totally acceptable to have one on
a random Tuesday afternoon in October.

Each element of this croissant includes rosewater, which can
be a pretty overpowering flavour, so you will note that the recipes
exercise restraint with respect to the addition of rosewater.

PERSIAN LOVE CAKE

300 g (10½ oz) blanched
almond meal

180 g (6⅓ oz) raw sugar

180 g (6⅓ oz) brown sugar

100 g (3½ oz) butter, fridge
cold, diced into small pieces

200 g (7 oz) Greek yoghurt

2 eggs

1 teaspoon ground nutmeg

PREPARE A DAY IN ADVANCE

1   Preheat your oven to 180°C fan (350°F). Grease a brownie tin
(27.5 × 17.5 cm/11 × 7 in) and line with baking paper.

2   In a bowl, combine the blanched almond meal, raw sugar, brown sugar
and cold butter and, using your fingertips, rub the ingredients together
to form a coarse crumb. This can also be done in a food processor, until
the ingredients just come together to form a homogenous crumb with no
obvious lumps of butter remaining.

3   Spoon 500 g (1 lb 2 oz) of the crumb into the prepared brownie tray
and distribute it evenly across the base of the tray, pressing down to create
a dense base (similar to the base of a cheesecake).

4   To the remaining crumb, add the Greek yoghurt, eggs and nutmeg
and mix together until you have achieved a smooth, homogenous batter.
Alternatively, the mix can be brought together quickly in a food processor.
If you are going down the food processor path, be careful not to overmix
the batter.

5   Pour the batter over the prepared base and tap the brownie tray
lightly on the benchtop to ensure the surface is nice and flat.

6   Bake for 30–35 minutes.

7   Remove from the oven and allow to cool to room temperature before
transferring to the fridge overnight to set completely.

8   The next day, remove from the tin and, using a ruler, portion into
4 × 7 cm (1½ x 2¾ in) slices. Store in a sealed container until you are ready
to assemble the Persian love cake croissant.

ROSEWATER SYRUP

500 g (17 oz) water

220 g (7¾ oz) caster
(superfine) sugar

1 tablespoon rosewater

1   Place the water and sugar in a small saucepan and stir over a medium
heat until all the sugar has dissolved, then allow the syrup to come to the
boil. Once boiling, remove from the heat and add the rosewater. →

ROSEWATER BUTTERCREAM

2 egg whites,
at room temperature

60 g (2 oz) water

200 g (7 oz) caster (superfine) sugar

250 g (9 oz) butter, at room temperature

1 tablespoon rosewater

3 drops of pink food colouring

1 In the bowl of a stand mixer fitted with the whisk attachment, whip the egg whites to soft peaks.

2 Meanwhile, bring the sugar and water to the boil in a small saucepan, stirring to dissolve the sugar and create a syrup. Using a candy thermometer, take the syrup to between 115 and 118°C (239 and 244°F).

3 Once the syrup has reached this temperature, remove from the heat and, in a slow and steady stream, carefully pour the sugar syrup into the egg whites while they are still whisking on low speed. Once all the sugar has been added, increase the speed of the mixer and whip until the bowl has cooled down to body temperature.

4 Cut the room-temperature butter into 2 cm (¾ in) pieces and begin gradually adding the butter to the whisking meringue, two or three pieces at a time, whisking well between each addition of butter to ensure that it is fully incorporated.

5 Once all butter is in, add the rosewater and pink food colouring and whisk to fully distribute the colouring. I would recommend adding two drops initially and checking the colour before adding the third. We're certainly not going for a hot pink garnish!

6 Transfer to a piping bag fitted with a size 11 star nozzle.

ASSEMBLING AND BAKING

1 Preheat your oven to 180°C fan (350°F) and line a large baking tray with baking paper.

2 Using a large serrated knife, cut the croissants in half. Brush the cut side of both halves of each croissant generously with the warm rosewater syrup. Pipe pistachio and rosewater frangipane to cover the bottom half of each croissant (not quite as much as you would for an almond croissant).

3 Place a slice of Persian love cake on top of the frangipane, pressing it down slightly to sink it into the frangipane.

4 Combine the pearl sugar and slivered pistachios in a medium bowl and stir to mix them up.

5 Replace the top half of each croissant, cupping your hand and gently securing each top. Finish each croissant off by piping a seam of pistachio frangipane across the top. Very carefully, holding the pastry from beneath, turn the croissant upside down and dip the seam of frangipane into the bowl of slivered pistachios and pearl sugar, pressing down to slightly flatten the frangipane and ensure that you get a nice amount of the pistachios and pearl sugar to stick.

6 Place the prepared croissants on the lined baking tray and bake for 20–25 minutes, until the frangipane inside is set.

7 Remove from the oven and allow to cool completely to room temperature, at least 30 minutes.

8 Once cooled, pipe 6 or 7 kisses of rosewater buttercream randomly over top of the pastry, then sprinkle dried rose petals over the buttercream kisses.

Leftovers

So you've committed to the whole three-day process, laboured over the rolling and folding and cutting and proving and baking, and now you've got more croissants than you know what to do with?

You've eaten more of them fresh out of the oven than you're going to admit to *anyone* (but I don't blame you, the pleasure of a croissant fresh from the oven is something I will *never* grow tired of), you've turned some of them into twice-baked Finger Bun croissants (good choice – I mean, how epic is the finger bun?!), but what to do with the *rest* of them?

Fear not, because leftover croissants can be used in a few applications that will transform a classic dish into an absolute showstopper.

Baked croissants store particularly well in Ziplock bags in the freezer, ready to be pulled out at a moment's notice to create a dinner party-worthy dessert, or simply turn your panzanella salad from good to exceptional.

Croissant 'Bread and Butter' Pudding

SERVES 10–12

6 day-old croissants

4 eggs

250 g (9 oz) milk

250 g (9 oz) thickened cream

1 teaspoon vanilla extract

30 g (1 oz) caster (superfine) sugar

Bread and butter pudding doesn't have a very glamorous ring to it, but, let me tell you, this pudding punches well above its weight. So much so that it was promoted to a Lune Lab dessert back in 2018.

As per the requirements for a Lune Lab dish, we didn't just serve up a scoop of pudding. We took a set slice of croissant pudding, fried it in beurre noisette, then coated it in vanilla sugar. It was served alongside house-made cultured cream and a blackberry compote.

Here I have given you the recipe for croissant 'bread and butter' pudding (which is incredibly delicious as it is; serve to dinner guests with a scoop of best quality vanilla ice cream and you'll have them licking their plates clean). There are also a few variations, should you feel so inclined to a little flavour twist to the base recipe.

ASSEMBLING

1   Grease a loaf tin and line with baking paper.

2   Tear the croissants roughly and arrange the pieces in the loaf tin.

3   Meanwhile, whisk the eggs, milk, cream, vanilla extract and sugar in a bowl to combine. Pour the egg mixture over the croissants and let stand for at least 1 hour, allowing the croissants to soak up the liquid.

4   Preheat your oven to 160°C fan (320°F). Bake the pudding in the oven for 45 minutes, or until a skewer inserted into the pudding comes out clean.

5   Leave to cool completely before turning out of the tin.

6   Cut into thick slices and serve in a puddle of runny cream.

THREE VARIATIONS

1   Instead of tearing the croissants into rough chunks, cut the croissants into slices and spread with hazelnut spread before arranging in the loaf tin. Proceed as per the recipe above.

2   For a Sicilian twist, as you are arranging the croissant pieces in the loaf tin, randomly distribute some ricotta and chopped dark chocolate among the croissant pieces. Add the grated zest of one orange to the egg mixture. Proceed as per the recipe above.

3   Warm 2 tablespoons of rum gently in a small pan, remove from the heat and add 100 g (3½ oz) of raisins. Allow to soak for 1 hour. Scatter the rum-soaked raisins among the croissant pieces. Add a pinch of freshly grated nutmeg to the egg mixture.

Chocolate-Dipped Croissant 'Biscotti'

MAKES MANY!

Sometimes you don't want a whole croissant with your coffee. Actually, I'm not crossing paths with any people that fit this description, so that's potentially a misnomer, but for the purposes of this recipe, let's pretend there are people out there that don't want a whole croissant with their coffee.

In Italy it's common to have a coffee and a biscuit for breakfast, hence why I've named this recipe Croissant 'Biscotti'. The texture of these thin, caramelised, double-baked slices of croissant are not dissimilar to biscotti, which is traditionally baked first as a large log of sweetened dough, the baked log then sliced into individual thins which are laid flat and baked again, resulting in that famed crunchy, dry texture (perfect for dipping in your coffee).

If you happen to have any croissants left over, this is a sensational little sweet snack to have stored in the pantry. And if you're like me, and you always want a whole croissant with your coffee, the best thing about these is that you don't have to stop at one …

CROISSANT 'BISCOTTI'

6 day-old croissants, frozen

500 g (1 lb 2 oz) thickened cream

300 g (10½ oz) caster (superfine) sugar, plus extra for sprinkling

4 teaspoons sea salt flakes

1   Preheat your oven to 150°C fan (300°F) and line a baking tray with baking paper.

2   Remove one croissant at a time from the freezer to keep the pastry as frozen and solid as possible. Slice a croissant in half lengthways through the nose and then, using a mandoline or a very sharp serrated knife, cut very thin slices of croissant widthways across each half.

3   Place the cream, sugar and salt in a saucepan and warm over a low heat, whisking to dissolve the sugar and salt.

4   Working one slice at a time, carefully pick up the croissant thins and coat them in the warmed cream, drain off any excess and arrange the slices in one layer on the lined baking tray.

5   Sprinkle the cream-coated slices with a little extra sugar and place in the oven to bake until they have reached a medium to dark golden brown colour. This will take longer than you expect. Start with 30 minutes on the timer and check them at the 30-minute mark. They may need a little longer to become really lovely and caramelised.

6   Cool completely, then transfer to a container until you are ready to dip them in the chocolate. →

TEMPERED CHOCOLATE

1 kg (2 lb 4 oz) dark chocolate (70% cocoa solids)

10 g (⅓ oz) cocoa butter

1 Set up a double boiler: bring 5 cm (2 in) of water to the boil in a medium saucepan then reduce heat to a simmer. Place a heatproof metal bowl over the top of the saucepan, ensuring that the bottom of the bowl isn't actually touching the water. Make sure that the bowl fits snugly, because if any condensation coming from the simmering water makes its way into the bowl, it will ruin the tempering of the chocolate.

2 Place 750 g (1 lb 10 oz) of the chocolate in the bowl with the cocoa butter and melt, monitoring the temperature. Once it reaches 50°C fan (122°F), carefully remove the bowl from the saucepan and gradually add the remaining 250 g (9 oz) of chocolate, stirring constantly with a clean, dry spatula and continuing to monitor the temperature. Adding the 250 g (9 oz) of chocolate will have reduced the temperature of the melted chocolate.

3 Reduce the temperature of the chocolate to 28°C (82°F), then place the bowl of melted chocolate briefly back over the saucepan, continually stirring, and bring the chocolate up to 32°C (89°F).

4 Your chocolate is now perfectly tempered and ready to use immediately.

FINISHING

1 Line a couple of baking trays with baking paper.

2 Take a cooled slice of croissant 'biscotti' and dip one end into the melted tempered chocolate. Twirl the piece of croissant around to allow any excess chocolate to drip off, then lay the slice of croissant onto one of the lined baking trays. Allow to set completely. If you have tempered your chocolate correctly, the surface of the set chocolate should be shiny, and the chocolate will snap when you break it or bite into it.

3 Repeat with the remaining slices of croissant biscotti.

4 Store in an airtight container in single layers, separated by baking paper.

CHEF NOTE You need to work very quickly to slice the croissants, as they don't take long to thaw out, and keeping them as solid as possible is the key to cutting even, thin slices.

Croissant Croutons

day-old croissants

olive oil, for drizzling

sea salt flakes

ground black pepper

Many cuisines, the world over, include dishes featuring some sort of a bread crouton.

Pieces of dried bread, or croutons, are the key ingredient in panzanella, the simple yet perfect Tuscan tomato and bread salad. Caesar salad utilises little crunchy croutons to add textural depth to a creamy, salty dish that masquerades under its healthy 'salad' banner (I mean, remove the cos lettuce and you basically have a deconstructed hangover fry-up). Fattoush, originating from Lebanon, uses leftover pita, fried and tossed with in-season chopped vegetables and herbs, often garnished with zingy sumac.

There are but three examples, and we've only considered the category of salads!

The myriad of soups that are likewise infinitely improved when garnished with a handful of croutons (I'm looking squarely at you, French onion), make this use of leftover croissants one of the easiest, yet most powerful kitchen weapons you can possess.

ASSEMBLING

1   Allow leftover croissants to rest for at least one night to become stale and dry out.

2   The following day, preheat your oven to 155°C fan (310°F). Cut each croissant into four or five large slices, then cut or tear the slices into rough pieces, approximately 2.5 cm (1 in).

3   Lay the pieces out on baking tray in a single layer, being careful not to overcrowd the tray. Drizzle the croissant pieces with olive oil, then season generously with sea salt flakes and pepper.

4   Bake for 15–20 minutes, tossing the croutons on the tray every 5 minutes, until they are crisp and reach a deep golden colour all over.

5   Allow to cool to room temperature before adding to your salad or soup of choice.

CHEF NOTE   Croissant croutons can be stored in an airtight container, but I would recommend using them immediately, for optimum crunch.

ESSENTIALS

The recipes that appear in this section are referenced multiple times throughout this book.

Frangipanes

ALMOND FRANGIPANE

200 g (7 oz) butter, at room temperature

200 g (7 oz) caster (superfine) sugar

grated zest of 1 orange

2 eggs

200 g (7 oz) natural almond meal

1   Beat the butter, sugar and orange zest in the bowl of a stand mixer fitted with a flat beater until pale and fluffy.

2   Add the eggs one at a time, continuing to beat and waiting until each one is incorporated fully before adding the next. Scrape down the bowl after incorporating the first egg.

3   With the mixer on low speed, mix in the almond meal. Once again, scrape the bowl down well, giving it a final mix by hand (with a spatula) to ensure all the ingredients are well incorporated.

4   Transfer the frangipane into a piping bag fitted with a size 11 star nozzle.

COCONUT FRANGIPANE

200 g (7 oz) butter, at room temperature

200 g (7 oz) caster (superfine) sugar

2 eggs

100 g (3½ oz) desiccated coconut

100 g (3½ oz) blanched almond meal

1   Beat the butter and sugar in the bowl of a stand mixer fitted with a flat beater until pale and fluffy. Add the eggs one at a time, continuing to beat and waiting until each one is incorporated fully before adding the next. Mix in the desiccated coconut and blanched almond meal. Transfer the frangipane into a piping bag fitted with a size 11 star nozzle.

PISTACHIO AND ROSEWATER FRANGIPANE

200 g (7 oz) butter, at room temperature

200 g (7 oz) caster (superfine) sugar

2 eggs

100 g (3½ oz) blanched almond meal

100 g (3½ oz) blanched pistachio meal

½ teaspoon rosewater

1   Beat the butter and sugar in the bowl of a stand mixer fitted with a flat beater until pale and fluffy. Add the eggs one at a time, continuing to beat and waiting until each one is incorporated fully before adding the next. Finally, mix in the rosewater, almond meal and pistachio meal. Transfer the frangipane into a piping bag fitted with a size 11 star nozzle.

PEANUT BUTTER FRANGIPANE

120 g (4¼ oz) butter, at room temperature

80 g (2¾ oz) smooth peanut butter

200 g (7 oz) caster (superfine) sugar

100 g (3½ oz) blanched almond meal

1   Beat the butter, peanut butter and sugar in the bowl of a stand mixer fitted with a flat beater until pale and fluffy. Add the eggs one at a time, continuing to beat and waiting until each one is incorporated fully before adding the next. Mix in the almond meal. Transfer the frangipane into a piping bag fitted with a size 11 star nozzle.

Crème Pâtissières and Custards

VANILLA CRÈME PÂTISSIÈRE

300 g (10½ oz) milk

½ vanilla pod, seeds scraped

4 egg yolks

50 g (1¾ oz) caster (superfine) sugar

10 g (⅓ oz) plain (all-purpose) flour, sifted

10 g (⅓ oz) cornflour (cornstarch), sifted

1 Heat the milk and vanilla in a saucepan to just below boiling point, taking care to not allow a skin to form.

2 Meanwhile, put the caster (superfine) sugar and egg yolks in a bowl and whisk well to combine, until the mixture is pale and light. Whisk in the plain (all-purpose) flour and cornflour (cornstarch) and whisk well again to combine.

3 When the milk is just about to boil, pour the milk gradually into the egg mixture, whisking constantly to incorporate. Now pour the egg and milk mixture back into the pan. Whisk the mixture continually over a medium heat until it begins to boil, and carry on whisking for about 3 minutes on the boil, until the crème pâtissière reaches a nice thick consistency.

4 Take off the heat and pour into a clean bowl. Place cling film over the surface of the crème pâtissière to prevent a skin from forming, then store in the fridge until ready to use.

PEANUT BUTTER CRÈME PÂTISSIÈRE

300 g (10½ oz) milk

½ teaspoon vanilla extract

50 g (1¾ oz) caster (superfine) sugar

2 eggs

1 tablespoon plain (all-purpose) flour

1 tablespoon cornflour (cornstarch)

50 g (1¾ oz) peanut butter

1 Heat the milk and vanilla extract in a saucepan to just below boiling point, taking care to not allow a skin to form.

2 Meanwhile, whisk the sugar and egg yolks in a bowl well until the mixture is pale and light. Add the plain (all-purpose) flour and cornflour (cornstarch) and again whisk well to combine.

3 When the milk is just about to boil, pour the milk gradually into the egg mixture, whisking constantly to incorporate. Now pour the egg and milk mixture back into the pan. Whisk the mixture continuously over a high heat until it begins to boil. Add the peanut butter. Continue to whisk for about 3 minutes on the boil, until the crème pâtissière reaches a nice thick consistency.

4 Take off the heat and pour into a clean heatproof bowl. Place cling film over the surface of the mixture to prevent a skin from forming, then let cool and reserve in the fridge until ready to use.

Other

SALTED CARAMEL

250 g (9 oz) cream

350 g (12 oz) caster (superfine) sugar

350 g (12 oz) butter at room temperature, cut into small cubes

8 g (0.3 oz) sea salt

1   Pour the cream into a small saucepan and bring to the boil, removing it from heat the moment it starts to boil.

2   Now take a clean, dry medium saucepan, and put it over a medium heat. Once the pan is hot, gradually sprinkle in some of your sugar, wait for it to melt, then sprinkle in a little more, waiting each time until all the sugar is melted before adding more. This technique allows you to have more control over the speed and evenness at which the sugar melts. Once the sugar is melted and evenly caramelised, reaching a deep brown consistency, remove from the heat and slowly pour in the hot cream, whisking continuously.

3   Let the caramel cool slightly, then add the butter a few pieces at a time, whisking them in until emulsified before adding more. Finally add the salt. Transfer to a bowl and refrigerate. Once completely cool, transfer to a piping bag.

DARK CHOCOLATE GANACHE

250 g (9 oz) dark chocolate buttons

37.5g (1⅓ oz) butter

18 g (¾ oz) liquid glucose

175 g (6 oz) thickened cream

1   Weigh the chocolate buttons, butter and glucose into a heatproof bowl.

2   Meanwhile, in a small saucepan, heat the cream until just below boiling point. I would recommend watching the cream, as it comes to the boil quickly!

3   Pour the cream over the prepared ingredients in the heatproof bowl and whisk until the mixture has a smoothy and glossy consistency.

DULCE DE LECHE

1 tin of sweetened condensed milk (typically 400 g/14 oz)

pinch of sea salt

PREPARE A DAY IN ADVANCE

1   Place the tin of sweetened condensed milk in a large saucepan, then fill the saucepan with water, such that it fully submerges the tin. Bring to the boil, then reduce the heat to a simmer and cook for 5–6 hours, checking intermittently that the water is always covering the tin (you will need to top up the water at intervals, so it's helpful to have your kettle boiled!).

2   After several hours in boiling water, carefully remove the tin with tongs and allow to cool completely. I would recommend boiling the tin the day before you want to use it and leaving it to cool completely overnight (we don't need anyone to get injured for the sake of a banoffee pie cruffin!).

3   The next day, open the tin and scoop out the beautifully caramelised filling into a mixing bowl. Add a pinch of sea salt and give the dulce de leche a good whisk to get a smooth consistency.

NAPPAGE

1 jar best-quality apricot jam
(Bonne Maman is my choice)

1 tablespoon water

1 tablespoon rum

1 Bring all the ingredients to the boil in a small saucepan over a medium heat. Strain through a sieve to remove any lumps of cooked apricot. Use while warm (as it cools down it will thicken up, making it harder to brush over pastry). If you are not going to use it immediately, nappage can be prepared in advance and stored in a sealed container in the fridge.

EGG WASH

1 1 egg, beaten and strained through a sieve (this will be enough for six pastries – if you are baking more than one of your batches of pastries, prepare more egg wash).

CINNAMON SUGAR

250 g (9 oz) caster (superfine) sugar

1 teaspoon ground cinnamon

1 Combine the sugar and cinnamon in a bowl, mixing thoroughly with a whisk to ensure that the cinnamon is evenly distributed. If you are dunking any of your pastries in the sugar and want to store the leftover sugar, sift it first, to remove any flakes of croissant pastry that may have found their way into it!

STRAWBERRY OR RASPBERRY JAM

400 g (14 oz) strawberries or raspberries
(fresh or frozen)

60 g (2 oz) caster (superfine) sugar

40 g (1½ oz) lemon juice

1 teaspoon vanilla extract

6 g (0.2 oz) pectin

pinch of salt

PREPARE A DAY IN ADVANCE

1 Place all the ingredients in a saucepan and bring to the boil, stirring frequently. Once the mixture has reached the boil, reduce the heat and allow to simmer for 30 minutes, again stirring regularly to ensure that it is not sticking to the bottom of the pan and burning.

2 Have a couple of sterilised jars at the ready, and once cooked, transfer the strawberry jam into the sterilised jars.

3 On the day you plan to make the finger buns or PBJ cruffins, transfer 150 g (5 oz) of strawberry jam into a piping bag. The rest can be stored in the fridge for up to 1 month.

INDEX

ACKNOWLEDGEMENTS

First and foremost, to my incredible Mum and Dad. You were my first ever staff members at Lune, and have been my biggest supporters from day dot (and that's my 'day dot', not just Lune's day dot!). I love you both very much, thank you for everything you do for me; each of my successess are your successes too.

To my bro, Cam. Together we have transformed my pursuit to make the perfect croissant into an iconic, but also viable, business. You have always had an unwavering dedication to the cause, a capacity to work harder than I've ever witnessed *anyone* work, the patience to put up with your *sister* for absurdly long days, weeks, months, under stressful and trying conditions. You also have the ability to make me laugh harder than anyone. Funny bugger.

You believed in me and this crazy little thing I'd started. You threw your full support behind Lune. You held my hand (metaphorically!) and helped me to slowly let go of control of all the areas I needed to in order to let little Lune grow into something magnificent. You've taught me so much. You brought your own style, and made your own enduring imprint on Lune, such that it is truly *ours*.

I'm so proud of you, and so lucky to be able to call you not only my business partner, but also my brother. I wouldn't change a single second of the last ten years.

To Chloe, Katie and Mitch, who helped me compile the recipes, many of which were developed before your times. I totally appreciate the challenge it would have been to pull together documentation that didn't actually exist! You were also so patient in answering my many questions about random ingredients, Thermomix alternatives for the home cook, and gelatine. Why did I have so many gelatine-related questions?! Chloe, Katie and Chelsea, thank you for the *enormous* effort you three put in over the days of the photoshoot - I think we can all agree that the results are simply stunning.

To all the chefs, present and past, who have brought their beautiful creativity, pastry skills and curious minds to Lune, and have contributed to the many brilliant pastries that have graced the counter of Lune.

To my best friend, Bianca, for literally checking in on me every day, encouraging me through the entire writing process, patiently bearing witness to many a recipe introduction that I impressed upon her. Promise I will never make you read a Lune recipe ever again! (Wouldn't want to be a mushy pear).

To my two favourite Melbourne clothing stores, Handsom and Somebuddy Loves You, for supplying some of the ridiculously delicious pieces featured in this book - I'm so grateful for your generosity and hope we did you proud!

To the epic creative team (pictured opposite) who have taken this incredible book journey with me. Evi – I can't believe I was lucky enough to do this with you. It was clear from the outset that our shared quirky view of the world was going to result in magic. Lee – on top of all your other styling talents, you have given me a new-found appreciation for napkin styling! Pete - my admiration for you just continues to grow. How you managed to make 60 croissant-like objects look this beautiful and unique is nothing short of a photographic miracle.

Finally, to Eve. Although you were on the other side of the world, from our very first zoom meeting, I knew there was no one else I wanted to create this book with. Thank you for your support, encouragement, expertise, guidance and trust. For being my biggest cheerleader AND my head test baker! You may have started out my Editor, but you've become my friend. X

Published in 2022 by Hardie Grant Books,
an imprint of Hardie Grant Publishing

Hardie Grant Books (London)
5th & 6th Floors
52–54 Southwark Street
London SE1 1UN

Hardie Grant Books (Melbourne)
Building 1, 658 Church Street
Richmond, Victoria 3121

hardiegrantbooks.com

All rights reserved. No part of this publication may be
reproduced, stored in a retrieval system or transmitted in
any form by any means, electronic, mechanical, photocopying,
recording or otherwise, without the prior written permission
ofthe publishers and copyright holders.

The moral rights of the author have been asserted.

Copyright text © Kate Reid
Copyright photography © Pete Dillon

British Library Cataloguing-in-Publication Data.
A catalogue record for this book is available from
the British Library.

Lune: Croissants All Day, All Night
ISBN: 978-1-78488-516-8
ISBN: 978-1-78488-622-6

10 9 8 7 6 5 4

Publishing Director: Kajal Mistry
Acting Publishing Director: Emma Hopkin
Commissioning Editor: Eve Marleau
Copy Editor: Laura Nickoll
Proofreader: Helen Graves
Design and Art Direction: Evi-O.Studio | Evi O.
Design Assistants: Evi-O.Studio | Kait Polkinghorne & Emi Chiba
Photographer: Pete Dillon
Production Controller: Nikolaus Ginelli

Colour reproduction by p2d
Printed and bound in China by Leo Paper Products Ltd.

MIX
Paper from
responsible sources
FSC™ C020056
www.fsc.org